Mind the Gap

THE CRACKS IN THE AMERICAN RETIREMENT
SYSTEM AND WHAT YOU CAN DO ABOUT THEM

Matthew C. Peck, CFP®

SHP Financial
PLYMOUTH, MASSACHUSETTS

Copyright © 2018 by Matthew C. Peck.

All rights reserved. No part of this publication may be reproduced, distributed or transmitted in any form or by any means, including photocopying, recording, or other electronic or mechanical methods, without the prior written permission of the publisher, except in the case of brief quotations embodied in critical reviews and certain other noncommercial uses permitted by copyright law. For permission requests, write to the publisher at the address below.

Matthew C. Peck/SHP Financial
225 Water Street, Building C
Suite C210
Plymouth, MA 02360
www.shpfinancial.com

Book Layout ©2013 BookDesignTemplates.com

Mind the Gap/ Matthew C. Peck. —2nd ed.
ISBN 978-1724466648

Contents

Acknowledgments i

Preface iii

Exposing the Gaps 1

Social Security 9

The Many Moving Parts of Medicare 25

Four Factors of Medicare 39

Bridging the Gaps in Long-Term Care 47

Long-Term Care Planning: Things You Need to Know 63

Minding the Income Gap with Modern Planning 85

Effective Income Solutions 101

Wealth is in the Eye of the Beholder 109

Setting and Striving for Clearly Defined Financial Goals 127

I dedicate this book to my beautiful wife of 11 years, Diana. Over the years her love and support while I work long hours have been irreplaceable. I was able to concentrate on my career while knowing that she was managing the home front and nurturing our four children.

I know I would not be the man I am today without her dedication, love and support.

Acknowledgments

I would like to express my gratitude to the many people who saw me through this project of updating the original 2013 version of "Mind the Gap". As they say, the one constant in life is change and after five years the old book needed to be updated.

Thank you to the original team who provided support through the many coffee-shop conversations and brainstorming sessions that ultimately helped shape my observations and opinions for these books. Truly, it was the invaluable wisdom and life experiences of my clients that I was able to combine with textbook knowledge to generate a real-world account of the pitfalls and opportunities of retirement.

Of course, this also includes my business partners, Derek Gregoire and Keith Ellis. It was their foresight that served as a catalyst to open SHP Financial's doors and develop it into the strong company it has now become. Innumerable lives have benefited from the financial planning and insight that my partners and staff have provided.

I appreciate the many individuals who allowed me to quote their remarks and assisted me in the editing, proofreading and design of this publication.

I would especially like to thank my copy editor, Tom Bowen, for helping me focus my prose and get the book from my mind into print and ready for publishing. I appreciate the valuable assistance of Jenny Herrick at Advisors Excel Creative Services, whose idea mill was consistent with my own in influencing creative ideas for this book.

I would be remiss if I did not mention Amazon Publishing and the fine work they did in assisting me with this project.

Preface

There are gaps everywhere you look. There are gaps in the sidewalk, gaps in the road, and small gaps in our windows sometimes where cold air seeps in during the winter. There are age gaps, philosophical gaps and communication gaps.

One of the most infamous gaps in history was the 18.5-minute gap in a tape-recorded conversation that took place in the Oval Office of the White House during the presidency of Richard M. Nixon. That little gap was the silence heard 'round the world during the Watergate investigation of the early 1970s.

Perhaps the most famous land mass gap is the American Grand Canyon. A little over a mile deep and 18 miles wide at its widest point, other chasms may be deeper and wider, but none has been visited, photographed and toured as much. Imagine the first humans who, trudging along on level ground, had their trek interrupted by that enormous gap, and how they must have felt as they pondered how to proceed.

In life, gaps are imperfections ... breaks in the seam ... interruptions along our intended pathway. To all but those who lead charmed lives, they are unavoidable, and they seem to appear when we least expect them.

The government has budget gaps. These are the holes in the nation's fiscal fabric that appear to be unreceptive to any of the patches that have been applied — those applied in recent years, anyway. Budget gaps are the result of the federal government spending more money than it takes in. These are gaps that seem to widen every year and show no sign of closure.

When it comes to our personal financial gaps, some of the more worrisome gaps are the empty spaces between what we hope to have, what we thought we had, and the reality of what we actually have in the end. The idea for the title of this book began as a kernel of thought about the gaps in our financial lives, our financial knowledge, how they impact us, and what we can do about them.

Personal financial gaps are occasionally the result of a work layoff or a job demotion, which suddenly leaves us staring at a new and unexpected gap — the one between our expenses and our income. Then there is the tuition gap, caused by the rising cost of obtaining a college education. This gap between financial aid and out-of-pocket expenses has forced many moms and dads to refinance their homes to cover the gap, which can be as high as $70,000 per year in some cases. Young people sometimes start their adult lives with a prosperity gap caused by student loan debt that seems to never go away.

It occurs to me that if life is a journey, you probably have a general idea where you are going, but the road sometimes takes you places that were not on your itinerary. You may be motoring along, enjoying the scenery, perhaps having one of those carefree, convertible-top-down-hair-blowing-in-the-wind moments, when the pavement abruptly ends and ahead of you is a cliff and a "Bridge Out" sign. That can be a bit scary.

The purpose of this book is to provide education on how to avoid the gaps in your financial journey if possible, and how to bridge them when you have to. Sometimes you have the resources to build that bridge, but you just don't know it. Other times, you need a map to help you find the detour. Every situation is different.

Retirement Gaps

Back in 2013 when I first wrote the book the goal was to educate and inform you, dear reader, on the retirement gaps, on how the entitlement programs work and more importantly where their help ends. We all need to know where our responsibility begins and over time this gap has only grown larger. In the private sector, the incessant march away from pensions and towards 401(k)s has not stopped and even pensions themselves are being bought out and pushed towards the consumer to manage. In the public sector, there has not been any action on fixing Social Security or getting the federal deficit under control. Whether we like it or not, it is our responsibility to know and to fix the gaps that are waiting for us. These could be the gaps in health care, income, investment returns, personal tax planning and estate planning. Yet the first step in filling these gaps is to fill the gap in our financial knowledge. The original book in 2013 was a step in that direction and I hope this updated revision will continue our journey towards that goal.

Some retirement gaps are still well known. There is the insurance known as "Medi-gap coverage," referring to health insurance purchased by those over age 65. It is designed to bridge the Medicare gap... to pick up where Medicare leaves off.

Other gaps are not so well known. Unfortunately, it is human nature to procrastinate and not face hard realities, which will include developing and sticking to a budget. In other words, the retirement gap that people are most unaware of is their income gap. What is the difference between what I need to spend to enjoy my retirement and my dedicated income streams?

Another serious gap that needs to be discussed is the long-term care gap, which could force you to spend thousands of dollars on the cost of home health care or skilled nursing home care. This money pit can siphon your resources until you are drained of everything you own. There is only so much you can do about the cracks in the sidewalks, the potholes in the street, or the increasing federal deficit, but there is a lot you can do about these retirement gaps, and it starts with knowing where they are.

Just like it is up to you to insulate and caulk your own home, many of the formidable gaps that are likely to confront you during your retirement years are essentially your responsibility. With the help of a professional who is skilled in such areas as home repair and insulation, you can successfully deal with the cracks and gaps in your physical house. Doing so sooner rather than later will eliminate unnecessary heating and cooling costs. It's the same with your retirement house. With proper planning and borrowing the skills and experience of a fully trained professional who has the right tools, you can eliminate the costly retirement gaps as well.

Medicare, Medicaid, Social Security

One goal of this book is to explore Medicare, Medicaid and Social Security, and how they interact with you and your retirement. All three are government-run entitlement programs that were neither designed for, nor intended to become, the answer to anyone's retirement problems. They were only intended to help, which is what they do. When it comes to health care, for example, Medicare was not designed to be umbrella coverage. It was intended to be a side benefit to assist with the rising health care cost for older Americans. It's the same thing with Social Security. It was never intended to be the sole support for seniors. It's a side fund. It was meant to be an adjunct to our personal savings program.

Medicaid (not to be confused with Medicare) was initially provided as a health care program for the indigent — the poor who could not help themselves. Although it is now used to pay for skilled nursing home care for millions of Americans, it was never designed for that purpose … nor is it the preferred choice for such care, since one has to achieve pauper status to qualify for it and settle for limited services.

It is clear, then, that there are gaps to be filled between what the government provides and what we can provide for ourselves. Knowing exactly what these government programs do and don't do and understanding how they fit into our overall retirement plan is crucial to building a sound retirement foundation. Social Security and Medicare are useful bricks in our foundation, but it would be a mistake to try to build a foundation with these bricks alone.

Straw, Sticks and Bricks

I can't help but recall the children's story of the three little pigs and how the first pig naively built his house of straw, which didn't last long against the big, bad wolf.

Some folks I have come across in my career as a Certified Financial Planner™ have that kind of problem with the structure, or lack of it, of their retirement plan.

The second pig did a little better. He used sticks, which, as everyone knows, have a bit more substance than straw, but don't perform much better as a building material. Similarly, some of us go into retirement with a plan that seems strong enough — that is, until the first adverse situation presents itself, such as a market downturn or excessive spending, and their plans collapse before our lupine monster can get out the second "f" in "puff."

The third pig had the good sense to use bricks. Solid stuff... wolf resistant. Likewise, some folks have solid retirement houses that are well constructed — built so as not to fail them for as long as they live. But it is a fact that relying only on the bricks provided by the government will leave you as vulnerable as our first two porcine pals when it comes to retirement planning. To properly fill the gaps, the first thing you need is lots more bricks... and the expertise to piece them together. It is my goal, through the pages of this book, to provide some insight in that regard.

During the time I have been helping people with their financial planning, I have discovered that knowledge is power, but only if it is put to work. Many of the clients I have worked with over the years have told me that they had no idea how many gaps there were to be filled — gaps not only in where the government ends and personal resources begin, but gaps in their understanding of how all the programs fit together. Hopefully this book will be of some assistance in pulling that picture together. I would like for as many as possible to enjoy their retirement and not have their retirement blown away by the predatory wolves of taxes, market volatility, spending, inflation, or catastrophic illness.

I am an avid hiker. A successful hike of any duration starts with planning. What you pack and the gear you take with you can make the difference between getting lost and making it to your goal. Like that hiker assembling his pack, I intend to give you the map, the compass, and all the directions you will need for a safe and successful journey. The rest, dear reader, will be up to you.

CHAPTER 1

Exposing the Gaps

"Your problem is to bridge the gap which exists between where you are now and the goal you intend to reach."
– Earl Nightingale

While on vacation in Mexico, a management consultant visited a small fishing village. He watched a little fishing boat dock at the wharf. Noting the quality of the fish, the consultant asked the fisherman how long it had taken to catch them.

"Not very long," answered the fisherman.

"Then why didn't you stay out longer and catch more?" asked the consultant.

The fisherman explained that his small catch was sufficient to meet his needs and those of his family.

The consultant asked, "But what do you do with the rest of your time?"

"I sleep late, fish a little, play with my children, and have an afternoon's rest under a coconut tree. In the evenings, I go into the village to play guitar with my friends, have a few beers, and sing a few songs. I have a full and happy life," replied the fisherman.

The consultant ventured, "I have an MBA from Harvard and I can help you. You should start by fishing longer every day. You can then sell the extra fish you catch. With the extra revenue, you can buy a bigger boat. With the extra money the larger boat will bring, you can buy a second one, a third one, and so on until you have a large fleet. Instead of selling your fish to a middleman, you can negotiate directly with the processing plants and maybe even open your own plant. You can then leave this little village and move to a city here, or maybe even in the United States, from where you can direct your huge enterprise."

"How long would that take?" asked the fisherman. "Oh, 10, maybe 20 years," replied the consultant.

"And after that?" asked the fisherman.

"After that? That's when it gets really interesting," answered the consultant, laughing. "When your business gets really big, you can start selling shares in your company and make millions!"

"Millions? Really? And after that?" pressed the fisherman.

"After that you'll be able to retire. You can sleep late, fish a little, play with your grandchildren, rest under a coconut tree, and, in the evenings, you can go into the village and play guitar with your friends, have a few beers, and sing a few songs."

Retirement Is a State of Mind

The reason why the story of the fisherman comes to mind is that we all see life through different lenses. All of us — me included — have a unique mental picture that appears when we hear the word "retirement." To some, the picture involves an idyllic life of leisure and solitude, to be far away from the maddening crowd. Others may embark on a new career or artistic pursuit that they had delayed during their working years but now are ready to commit to pursuing. Others who are more gregarious may see themselves surrounded by people — the more the merrier! Some see themselves traveling to far-flung places. Others just want to enjoy being at home, playing with their grandchildren and gardening. Different strokes for different folks, as they say.

But one thing is certain. Any retirement scene will be more enjoyable without the cloud of financial uncertainty hovering overhead.

One truth of the illustration of the fisherman is this: How we spend our working years can affect the years we spend in retirement. While the fisherman surely enjoyed his lot in life and was content, the management consultant clearly had another vision. In the end, the fisherman landed back where he started, but probably with a thicker wallet and a bigger bank account. It is also a lesson to us financial planners, too. What is most important to the client is most important, period. Our view of retirement success may not be the same as that viewed through the prism of the client. I am convinced that very few people think about money when they flash on that word, "retirement." They may daydream about the measure of leisure that money will provide them, but they don't conjure images of bills and coins or numbers on a balance sheet. As an old saying goes, "You'd like to have an exciting retirement but a boring portfolio."

What is your vision of your retirement? Where will you spend your time, and what will you be doing after you have finished your time in the workplace?

Baby Boomers Retiring

The generation of baby boomers that survived the economic crash of 2008 essentially had the rug ripped from under them when the stock market plummeted. Many lost more than 50 percent of their retirement in the markets. Add to that a ballooning government debt and the threat of a failing Social Security program, and we can see why many no longer look at retirement as the worry-free safe haven they thought it would be. In fact, many people in their 50s and 60s are planning to work until they turn 70 out of concern for their retirement and the lack of support that Social Security will be able to provide. It is this helpless feeling that is very common among the people who walk through our doors and feel that they'll never be able to retire.

For so many boomers — a generation that values youth — visions of an early retirement faded quickly when they saw the money they worked so hard to stash away disappear so suddenly. Many of you who are reading this book are probably members of the baby boom generation — those born between 1946 and 1964. The name originates from the spike in the birth rate after soldiers returned from World War II and began finding jobs and starting families. As a generation, boomers are a progressive lot. They have accomplished much and are still forging a record of achievement and advancement, the likes of which the world has never seen. If you are a baby boomer, much of what follows will strike a chord with you. If you are reading this book and you are not a member of the boom generation because you were born after 1964, then high five to you. You will still appreciate some of the information because your time is coming, and planning for it should start as early as possible. You should implement some of the strategies you see here as well. If you were born prior to 1946, then please stay tuned, because much of what you read will apply to you as well.

It has been said that boomers are the highest-earning generation in the history of our nation and have proved to their children that it is possible to accumulate wealth. Most boomers are still in the "accumulation phase" of their lives; they are still in their working years, earning an income and gathering money into their storehouses for later use when they retire. Some are accumulating too much debt and too many toys for their own good, but we will talk about that later.

The accumulation phase is the precursor to the "distribution phase." This phase begins when you leave work and retire. The "distribution phase," as the term implies, is when you stop accumulating wealth and start distributing what you have accumulated — using those funds to write your own "paycheck," so to speak.

An interesting thing happened on January 1, 2011. The first baby boomer turned 65. As the oldest members of the baby boom generation celebrated their 65th birthday, the retirement stampede began. According to the Pew Research Center, every day, for the next 19 years, 10,000 people will reach age 65. If boomers represent 26 percent of the total U.S. population, you can just imagine how that will change, and is changing, the social and economic landscape of the country. Don't tell baby boomers that they are old, however. A Pew Research Center survey revealed that the typical boomer thinks old age doesn't begin until 72. According to their findings, fully half the adults said they feel nine years younger than their chronological age.

As the largest retiring generation ever, boomers bring a unique perspective to retirement. The generation that brought us rock and roll and Woodstock was also responsible for the economic boom of the 1990s. They gave us the Internet, too. Boomers started their own businesses in record numbers. They spend more money and time on leisure activities than any generation before them. "Work hard and play hard" has been their mantra.

The old image of a husband and wife sitting around the house after age 60 is anathema to modern retirees. That kind of drudgery is hardly the kind of retirement that members of this idealistic generation worked so hard to achieve. That antiquated image has been replaced with new-age world travelers and senior citizens enjoying the thrill of starting a "fun" business as a second career.

Some of these new businesses may be started out of necessity. But many hip oldsters are starting businesses for the first time in their lives. During their younger years, there was too much on the line; now that they are older, they are eager to take a chance at beginning a new career.

Travel is high on the list for many of these new retirees. They are heading for exotic places in droves and taking their cash with them. These dreamers are now doers.

One reality, however, that must be faced is that to maintain such a high profile in retirement requires financial resources. If you were earning six figures before you retired, and you wish to continue living the same lifestyle in retirement, then those dollars must continue to roll in. If you have already arranged for this and it presents no problem for you, then I hold my glass high in a salutatory toast to you because you are one of the fortunate few. As a financial planner specializing in retirement counseling, most of those with whom I come in contact need a lot of help in bridging that prosperity gap. Sometimes a reality check takes place between the retirement that had been envisioned and the one that can be afforded.

As I work with retirees and pre-retirees every day, a common theme keeps coming up in our conversations — how quickly time flew by and how unprepared they still felt they were. I share this with you younger readers to underscore the fact that it is never too early to start planning. It is also never too late to plan, either. At any stage of life, having a good financial plan can provide a purpose to each one of your assets and provide direction for where to apply your savings. Moreover, a good financial plan provides the confidence that you need when entering retirement that you have crunched numbers and know the long-term consequences of what you are spending, your tax consequences, the impact on inflation, and so. Too often people enter retirement without a plan and do not have a well-researched answer to questions like. "Can I take that trip?' Can I give that gift to my grandchild? Can I help towards their college education?" Without a good plan, retirement can be a scary place. But it doesn't have to be. For example, there are many resources available to modern retirees that were not there for earlier generations.

Planning is more important than it used to be. Unless you have been living under a rock for the last 30 years, you know that the once simple retirement plan of working for the same company for 30 years, leaving with a substantial pension, and using Social Security to supplement your pension's retirement income is no longer a realistic option. In fact, pension plans are almost nonexistent these days. Social Security? There are those who predict that it, too, will be nonexistent before the boomers have all retired. We will dive deeper into that in the next chapter when we discuss the Social Security gap.

Properly done, retirement planning goes way beyond what we used to know about retirement. It goes further than what any government program could ever provide. It looks at what your goals are and how to get there. Planning properly requires knowledge and education in order to choose the right vehicle to take you to your financial destination.

Social Security, Medicare and Medicaid leave gaps, and we must confront them, just as we would confront any other continuity lapse. But they have their own merits, to be sure, as we will see in future chapters. They are bricks, just not the only bricks, in our financial foundation.

CHAPTER 2

Social Security

"If you want total security, go to prison. There you're fed, clothed, given medical care, and so on. The only thing lacking ... is freedom."
— Dwight D. Eisenhower

The idea of a "retirement age" is relatively new. Nothing has done more to define and influence retirement as we know it than the Social Security Act, passed under the administration of Franklin D. Roosevelt in 1935, where it was first put forth that 65 was the appropriate age at which to retire. Interestingly, when the Social Security program was initiated in 1935, the average life expectancy was 61 years.

Considering that the average age for retirement has remained consistently around 65, beneficiaries in the early years of the program were receiving payment for a much shorter time.[1] So the people who wrote the Social Security Act and the lawmakers who enacted the legislation probably never intended for the program to

---

[1] Moon, Marilyn and Mulvey, Janemarie. Urban Institute Press. 1996. "Entitlements and the Elderly: Protecting Promises, Recognizing Reality,." pg. 27.
https://web.stanford.edu/class/e297c/poverty_prejudice/soc_sec/hsocialsec.htm

pay out very much money, did they? They certainly would have never expected that it would be a source of income for millions of Americans who would live well into their 90s. Some say that, had this law been enacted in the 21st century, the retirement age would have been set at 80, and they are probably right.

Money started flowing into the Social Security trust in 1937, two years after the passage of the Act. Under the Reagan administration, the federal government modified the retirement age to 67 for those born after 1960. No other age reforms have been made in the last 30 years.

Social Security was designed to be a safety net for older Americans. It was never designed to cover all their living expenses. But according to The Motley Fool, an internet stock market watch organization, an estimated 61 percent of retirees rely on their benefits to provide at least half of their income.[2]

The U.S. Social Security Administration reports that in 2018, about 63 million Americans will receive approximately $1 trillion in Social Security benefits and that Social Security benefits represent about one-third of the income for the elderly. Half of all married couples and 71 percent of all single people on Social Security consider their monthly check from the government to represent half their total income.[3]

This reliance on Social Security has both financial and political ramifications. Financially, retirees across the country are being crushed by outside costs such as health insurance and inflation. They struggle month to month, surviving only on their government checks. Politically, this reliance has directly caused the

---

[2] Backman, Maurie. The Motley Fool. June 26, 2017. "Can the Average American Live Off Social Security?"
https://www.fool.com/retirement/2017/06/26/can-the-average-american-live-off-social-security.aspx

[3] Social Security Administration. "2017 Social Security Fact Sheet."
https://www.ssa.gov/news/press/factsheets/basicfact-alt.pdf

program to become a standard "third rail" of politics. Any suggestion to alter the program generates enormous spin and backlash. Just the mention of tampering with Social Security seems to set off fireworks of protest. President George W. Bush began advocating privatizing Social Security soon after he was elected, and began pushing the idea in earnest in 2005, following his reelection the year before. His idea was that money invested in the private sector would result in a greater payout during old age than would money paid into a government-run program. But the idea failed to gain much momentum. Even though his plan would have affected only younger workers, senior citizens lobbied hard to ensure that not one single hair of the program was changed.

Because so large a portion of retirees rely on their Social Security income to survive, political observers seem to be of the opinion that Social Security reform will never see the light of day until the handwriting on the wall becomes painfully obvious that the ship has run hard aground. In the current political climate, to suggest a change in Social Security is to touch the eyeball of older Americans and, if you are a politician, spells an end to your hopes of getting elected to any office higher than dog catcher.

Disturbing news comes from those who crunch the numbers. Some of them are telling us that, with so many baby boomers retiring, it is only a matter of time before the program goes broke.

"The future of Social Security remains uncertain," writes financial reporter Cameron Huddleston, "leaving people with Social Security asking questions like, 'Will Social Security run out?'"

Huddleston points out that the 2017 annual report of the SSA Board of Trustees acknowledges that the Trust Fund's income is expected to exceed its expenses only until 2034. After that, projected annual taxes are expected to cover only about 75 percent of the benefits in following years.[4]

Problematic for Social Security is the fact that baby boomers are leaving the workforce and fewer of working age are replacing them, leaving insufficient funding to support those who retire. A massive fall in revenue from the payroll tax, known as the Federal Insurance Contributions Act (FICA), occurred during the Great Recession of 2008, shrinking the flow of money into the program, while the outflow of money from the program continued to increase. Additionally, a report from the Centers of Disease Control and Prevention in 2018 showed the lowest number of births in the U.S. in 30 years. If there are less workers paying into the system, this further stresses the current structure. All in all, anyone who is 40 years old or younger and planning to rely on Social Security for any significant portion of their financial needs in retirement should keep an eye on this situation.

Minding the Gap

From a world view, the state of our federal government and its growing debt must be considered when we discuss the viability of Social Security. At first, I debated with myself as to whether to include this, but if we are going to be real about minding the gaps in retirement, the true state of things needs to be exposed.

When the federal government releases budget and debt figures, it does not include Social Security and the implied promises that have been made to generations of Americans. This means that the government is not listing Social Security as a debt. If it were to do

---

[4] Huddleston, Cameron. GoBankingRates. April 4, 2018. "What Social Security Will Look Like in 2035." https://www.gobankingrates.com/investing/what-will-social-security-be-in-2035

so, then trillions of dollars would have to be added to the deficit column of the balance sheet.

Interestingly, the standard framework of guidelines used to calculate the nation's debt is referred to as the Generally Accepted Accounting Principles, or GAAP. GAAP is the rule book that CPA firms and corporations go by when creating a report to show how well or how poorly an entity or enterprise is doing financially. Following Generally Accepted Accounting Principles, you shouldn't be able to "cook the books," so to speak, or compile bogus information in an effort to fool the stockholders, or, in the case of the government, the general public.

Unfunded Liabilities

One of the scariest monsters hiding under the beds of future retirees goes by the name of "Unfunded Liabilities." What's that? One financial terms glossary defines it this way: "The amount, at any given time, by which the future payment obligations exceed the present value of funds available to pay them."

Pension plans (such as Social Security and Medicare) have certain contractual obligations – income benefits, death benefits, etc. Those are liabilities. If the pension plan's projected assets cannot cover them, they are "unfunded liabilities."

Financial writer and Forbes contributor John Mauldin claims the amount of unfunded government liabilities has soared into the trillions of dollars. He cites a table on page 63 of the Financial Report for the United States Government for fiscal year 2016 that reveals the net present value of the government's 75-year future liability for Social Security and Medicare. Liabilities exceed present value of tax revenue designated to pay those benefits by a whopping $46.7 trillion, claims Mauldin.

"Where will this $46.7 trillion come from?" the writer asks. "We don't know. Future congresses will have to find it somewhere."[5]

Is the situation improving? Not from where I watch the world. According to financial information website MarketWatch, the federal government ran a budget deficit of $666 billion in fiscal 2017 (the biggest shortfall since 2013) and finished fiscal year 2017 with a budget deficit of $666 billion, an increase of $80 billion over the previous year.[6]

Think of unfunded liabilities this way: If you were to keep a ledger of your personal expenditures for the month, would you count what you spend in cash as well as those purchases for which you used the credit card? Of course, you would. Although the credit card purchases represent transactions where you promise to pay later, they are still expenditures. While that makes perfect sense to you and me, the US government does not count "promises to pay later," which is what Social Security and Medicare are, when calculating budget deficits.

As the Congressional Budget Office pointed out, the budget deficit for the year 2018 was officially $804 billion,[7] but when you add in the rise in liabilities for the nation's retirement programs, that adds another $1.6 trillion to the total. Why should we call that a debt? Because those are future financial promises that we have made that future taxes are not expected to cover.

---

[5] Mauldin, John. Forbes. October 10, 2017. "Your Pension Is a Lie: There's $210 Trillion of Liabilities Our Government Can't Fulfill."
https://www.forbes.com/sites/johnmauldin/2017/10/10/your-pension-is-a-lie-theres-210-trillion-of-liabilities-our-government-cant-fulfill/#152f8fda65b1

[6] Schroeder, Robert. Marketwatch. October 20, 2017. "U.S. ends fiscal 2017 with $666 billion budget deficit." https://www.marketwatch.com/story/us-ends-fiscal-2017-with-666-billion-budget-deficit-2017-10-20

[7] Congressional Budget Office. "Budget." https://www.cbo.gov/topics/budget

When to Take Benefits

In no way do I intend in this book to take you down the rabbit hole and explore every one of the endless options that are being floated on how to fix Social Security. Most of them boil down to either cutting benefits or extending the age at which participants may qualify to receive them, or a combination of the two. And, as distasteful as that may be to some, it will likely save the program. The good news for most baby boomers is that any changes are not likely to affect them.

What will affect them is the question of when to take Social Security benefits. I had one client tell me that he was taking his benefits early. Not because he was in ill health, but because he believed that when the government does make what he feels are inevitable changes to the Social Security system, they will be less likely to change the rules for current beneficiaries. He thinks taking his benefits now will enable him to be "grandfathered," and thus immune to any cuts. I couldn't argue with his logic, but I don't advise anyone to rush to take early benefits without careful consideration.

Remember when, during the 2012 presidential campaign, Governor Rick Perry of Texas called the Social Security system a "Ponzi scheme?" Charles Ponzi was an Italian con man who became known in the early 1920s as a swindler in North America for his money-making scheme of promising clients unreasonably high and unbelievably quick returns on their investments. He was actually paying early investors with the money received from later investors.

Depending on how harsh you want to be in your definition, the comparison may not be too unjustified. With Social Security, the growth of payouts depends on the growth of the number of future taxpayers, or future investors. But by that definition, private investment accounts — the ones that reform conservatives are proposing as a replacement for Social Security, or at least an alternative to it — are Ponzi schemes as well. The only difference is whether we want the government or the public sector to administer the plan. Either way, the constant in the equation is that today's income will still depend on tomorrow's contributions. Let's not forget that the government can print money.

I like to explain Social Security as a fixed annuity that is run by the federal government and funded by current workers. While many who agree with the Ponzi scheme label point out that we are taking from one group (the workers) to pay the other group (retirees, the disabled, and widows), there is more to it than that. If we focus solely on retirement and how the benefits are paid, I think you will see what I mean.

There are many different annuities — fixed, variable, fixed index, Medicaid, etc. One type of annuity is called a Single Premium Immediate Annuity (SPIA). Certain SPIAs are called "life only," which means that you deposit a large amount of money into an account, which then pays a certain amount per month for the rest of your life. When you pass away, there is nothing remaining.

Once you open this "life only" SPIA, the payments that create the income stream are based on your life expectancy. Since the payments will continue for the rest of your life, your age will determine what the amount of those payments will be.

Social Security income works in a similar way. Naturally, the later you begin taking those payments, the lower your life expectancy and the higher your income base will be. With Social Security, you periodically receive COLAs (Cost of Living Adjustments). These increases will be that much higher because it is a percentage of your base.

Here's an example. Let's say Steve, who is single with no dependents, is considering retirement options at age 66 versus age 70. His income base at age 66 is $2,400 per month. His income base at age 70 is $3,200 per month. If he starts at age 66, and his COLA is three percent, his income goes up $72 at age 67. But if he waits until age 70 to take the $3,200 per month, the 4 percent increase would be $96, so his monthly income would rise to $3,296 the next year. In other words, not only are you getting an average 8 percent increase in your base monthly amount by delaying (which is guaranteed by the federal government, mind you), but when they add COLA to your base monthly amount, you're adding a percentage on a higher number; hence, the difference in the monthly income of $72 versus $96.

All future increases would be based on the new amount. It is all a percentage. The percentage amount stays the same, but the increase per month is dramatically different based on the income base.

Yet the decision when to start taking your Social Security benefits is not as cut and dried. There are other factors to consider. My job would be all too easy if I just sat in my comfy desk chair and told people when to take their Social Security income. But every situation is different. The ideal financial plan-by-the-numbers scenario may not mesh with the ideal financial plan that meets your individual needs. Reality sometimes must be accommodated.

Let's take a closer look at the additional realities to be considered when determining the best time for you to take your Social Security benefits.

The Break-Even Age

It would be helpful if we could have a crystal ball by our side with every decision we had to make. The decision of when to take Social Security would be an easy one. But no one knows what the future holds, and there are no guarantees. We can, however, apply some math to the matter. There is something called the "break-even age." This is the age to which you would have to live in order for the numbers to fall in your favor. If you elected to take your Social Security benefits at age 62 instead of waiting until age 70, for example, to what age would you have to live in order to receive more than you paid into the system during your working years?

Remember the number 77. Putting aside cost of living increases, by taking your Social Security at age 62, you are ahead of the game and earning more money for the first 15 years. After age 77, the precipitous slide begins. You now start earning less money. The longer you live, the worse the decision to take early benefits becomes.

Consider this chart that maps the potential benefit earnings at different starting years. Unequivocally, the later you start your payments, the more you earn each year past age 77. And this is with no cost of living adjustment included. However, let us consider one more argument on the taking Social Security early side of things: If you were to smartly reinvest the early monthly payments from Social Security, you may be able to push back the inevitable break-even age but this assumes that you do not spend the money or need the money. Setting that argument aside, let's look at the following chart from a pure monthly income perspective:

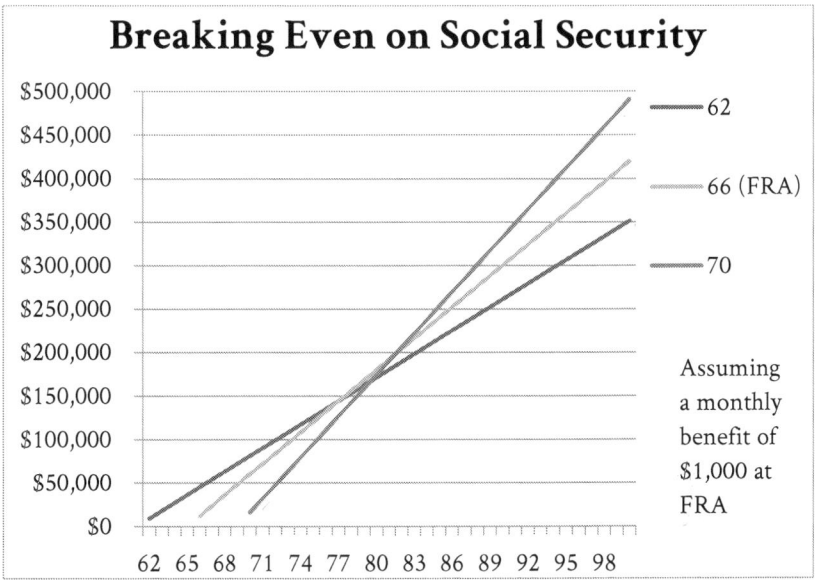

Health

With the break-even age of 77-82 fresh in our minds, the critical question we have to ask ourselves becomes, "How long am I going to live?" Such an existentialist question is impossible to answer. When you are considering your decision as to whether to start your Social Security income, it is best to give yourself a frank and honest assessment. Think about your current health and the longevity of your parents. With a reasonable amount of logic and common sense, you should be able to know how confident you feel about living until age 77.

Let's say that I had an uncle who was a chain-smoking alcoholic and was in such poor health that by age 62 every new dawn he experienced was a bonus. If I were to advise him, based solely on his

---

[8] Estimates based on Social Security data for someone born Jan. 10, 1949 with base wage earnings at or exceeding the Social Security minimum.

health, as to when he should take Social Security to get the most out of the benefits, I would probably tell him to start the checks rolling in as soon as possible. Someone who is the picture of health, however, and can wait until his or her full retirement age, it would probably be in his or her best interests to do just that.

I use the word "probably" here because the most frustrating part of these two scenarios is that we just don't know what tomorrow will bring. Most people have the experience of a friend or colleague who is in great health, but suddenly drops dead. I have experienced this first-hand. Ohers who spent their lives abusing their bodies live well into their 90s. Life is as unfair as it is unpredictable.

Consider your parents. If you reach age 62 and your parents are still alive, chances are you have a very good probability of making it beyond age 77. In that instance, waiting to start payments might be prudent. Advancements in medicine also play a part. What was killing our parents may now be treated if detected early. Because of advancements in medical technology, and because of better lifestyle habits and more exercise, people are living longer these days.

Working Income, Social Security, and the IRS

One sound reason to wait on your Social Security check is the "withholding" rule. Can you get Social Security retirement benefits while you continue to work? Sure, you can. But if you aren't full retirement age (age 66 for most folks as of 2018), and you earn more than the yearly limit, Social Security will reduce your benefit by $1 for every $2 you earn above the annual limit. The limit was $17,040 as of 2018. When you reach full retirement age, they will not reduce your benefits no matter how much you earn. See why it may be prudent to wait to take your Social Security benefits if you plan to continue working?[9]

As I see it, if you are able to work and you want to work, then your health is probably pretty good. This means that delaying your Social Security income payments will probably be in your best interests. The folks who really should be careful are the ones who decide to retire, take early payments, and then have to come out of retirement for one reason or another. Unless you are Brett Favre, coming in and out of retirement could have negative financial consequences. Favre, a famous quarterback for the Green Bay Packers from 1992 to 2007, might just hold the record for retiring and unretiring, having hung up his cleats in 2007, 2009, 2010, and finally, it appears, for good in 2011.

Many of my clients will continue to work for both financial and mental reasons. Not only will these clients delay Social Security due to the earned income limit, but also because of the taxation of these benefits. Why begin taking income from Social Security if that means that all of their earned income may push them into a new tax bracket and increase Uncle Sam's cut?

Now the good news is that Social Security has a tiered system as to how much is taxable, with a limit being 85 percent of the monthly benefit. The calculation is based on what Social Security calls the "base amount" or "combined income," which is different from other calculations. For Social Security, it is as follows: 'adjusted gross income + nontaxable interest + half of your Social Security benefits.'[10]

---

[9] Social Security Administration. 2018. "How Work Affects Your Benefits." https://www.ssa.gov/pubs/EN-05-10069.pdf

[10] Josephson, Amelia. SmartAsset. June 28, 2018. "Is Social Security Income Taxable? https://smartasset.com/retirement/is-social-security-income-taxable

SOCIAL SECURITY TAXATION

	Individual	Married Filing Jointly
Not taxable	Less than $25,000	Less than $32,000
Up to 50% taxable	$25,000 to $34,000	$32,000 to $44,000
Up to 85% taxable	Greater than $34,000	Greater than $44,000

Be aware of what your working income would do to this calculation as well as your other income sources; all combine to become a major factor as to when you elect to take Social Security. If you think that you may want to continue working after reaching retirement age, you will definitely want to delay taking your Social Security payments until you make up your mind.

Spouse

The final factor to consider when deciding whether to take early payments has to do with your spouse. What is his or her Social Security situation? Is your spouse's benefit higher than yours? Will he/she have a higher benefit in the future? When one spouse passes away, the surviving spouse begins receiving the higher Social Security payment amount, not both.

For example, in a typical middle-income household, a couple is nearing retirement age. The husband is earning a Social Security income of $2,000 per month. The wife's Social Security income is $1,000 per month. If either the husband or the wife dies, the $1,000 monthly income from the wife's Social Security will disappear, leaving the surviving spouse with the $2,000 per month. This plays an important role, because if your personal payments are scheduled to be the higher payment, then deferring these payments is in your best interests. Not only are you increasing your own personal income base and the additional Cost of Living Adjustment, but you are increasing the income base for your spouse, if you were to die before him or her.

On the flip side to aiming for the higher income, if you know your scheduled payments are going to be lower than those of your spouse, taking early payments is a good bet. Since your smaller payments are going away upon the death of either you or your spouse, it matters less if you decide to begin your Social Security income at age 62.

Another option to consider is the 50 percent rule, which pertains to deferring your own personal payments and taking 50 percent of your spouse's payments. This option, like many of the options discussed above, is based on many factors, which may not be readily apparent. For example, certain selections are only available if both spouses have filed.

All of this may seem confusing and a little morbid. No one wants to think about his or her own death or the death of a spouse. But from a financial perspective, it is important to understand these nuances of Social Security that come with retirement planning.

Conclusion

In a world of less pensions, Social Security income is the one guaranteed lifetime payment that you'll have and maximizing the return should be a major goal of your financial plan. If you are able to smartly maximize your Social Security income, you have made a large step in closing the eventual income gap that will open once your working income stops.

We don't know exactly how long Social Security is going to be around. We do know that we are paying into this fund that is supposed to help us when it is time for us to retire from our careers. Will we ever see that money again? It depends on our current age and the government's ability to repair the cracks in the program's foundation.

However, for those of us who are nearing retirement age, there are several factors to consider when it comes to when we activate our Social Security benefits. Avoid the tendency to follow the herd or take the advice of well-meaning friends or relatives. Every situation is different. Analyze the decision by considering everything that could affect your financial situation and your overall retirement picture.

CHAPTER 3

The Many Moving Parts of Medicare

> "The Great Society is a place where every child can find knowledge to enrich his mind and to enlarge his talents. It is a place where the city of man serves not only the needs of the body and the demands of commerce, but the desire for beauty and the hunger for community. It is a place where men are more concerned with the quality of their goals than the quantity of their goods."
> – Lyndon B. Johnson

In May 1964, President Lyndon B. Johnson gave a speech at the University of Michigan in Ann Arbor in which he outlined his domestic agenda for the United States. He applauded the nation's wealth and abundance. President Johnson then warned the audience, "The challenge of the next half-century is whether we have the wisdom to use that wealth to enrich and elevate our national life, and to advance the quality of American civilization." Johnson's agenda was based on his vision of what he called "The Great Society," the name by which the agenda became popularly known.

Part of the Great Society agenda was based on initiatives proposed by Johnson's predecessor, John F. Kennedy, but Johnson's vision was more comprehensive and far reaching. Johnson wanted to use the resources of the federal government to combat poverty, strengthen civil rights, improve public education, revamp urban communities, and protect the country's natural resources.

During this Great Society of the 1960s, the push to use government resources also included a push to strengthen the health insurance system and the social safety net for the neediest of individuals. The answer was Medicare and Medicaid. These two programs were the basis of the government-run Center of Medicare and Medicaid Services (CMS). We will explore Medicaid in a future section as it relates to nursing homes and long-term care, and how to plan around the gaps it leaves.

Since its inception, Medicare has been a lightning rod for controversy. Every two years, as the election cycle spins, Medicare becomes the perfect topic for the intraparty blame game. In recent years, some government proposals affecting Medicare have either been enacted or put on the table that have caused no small degree of imbalance to the system. In 2010, the Patient Protection and Affordable Care Act, also known as "Obamacare," was passed. This act directly impacted Medicare, with part of the expenses going to close the Part D coverage gap, or the "donut hole," as it is popularly known, in prescription drug coverage. I will go over more details on Part D later in this chapter.

In 2011, Congressman Paul Ryan of Wisconsin unveiled his "Path to Prosperity." If enacted, this proposal would revolutionize Medicare. It would shift the burden of Medicare from the federal government to private industry and citizens. The stated aim of this proposal is to cut the federal deficit and let the free markets control health care costs.

Every year there are going to be actions, or calls to action, that may or may not affect Medicare. My job in this book is not to speculate about what the future of Medicare may be, but rather to focus on the system as it currently stands and provide strategies to help you navigate through it.

Part A — Hospital Coverage

Medicare Part A is your hospitalization coverage, or as I like to call it, the roof over your head and hospital bed. Practically everyone who has put in his or her 40 quarters (10 cumulative years) of paying into the program will automatically go into Medicare Part A, without a monthly premium, upon turning 65. At age 65, you qualify for Medicare if you:

- Receive Social Security or railroad retirement benefits;
- Have worked long enough to be eligible, but are not getting Social Security or railroad retirement benefits;
- Would be entitled to Social Security benefits based on your spouse's (or divorced spouse's) work record, and that spouse is at least 62 (your spouse does not have to apply for benefits in order for you to be eligible based on your spouse's work); or
- Worked long enough in a federal, state or local government job to be insured for Medicare.

If you are under age 65, you may be able to qualify for Part A if you get Social Security disability benefits and have Lou Gehrig's disease, have been receiving Social Security disability for 24 months, or if you have worked long enough in a federal, state or local government job to meet the program's requirements.

The bottom line is you have to qualify.

Once you have qualified, under Part A, all the services that are required during a hospitalization are covered. This includes necessary surgeries, around-the-clock nursing care, semiprivate room, food, IVs, and so on. Basically, any care and comfort you receive when you are actually admitted to the hospital will be covered by Medicare Part A, minus deductibles and co-pays.

As of this writing, the deductible for Part A is $1,340 for each benefit period. This means that if an individual only has Part A, without a supplement or Medicare Advantage Plan (Part C), then he or she is responsible for paying the $1,340 for each visit to the hospital, or, as the Medicare language puts it, "each medical episode." What is a medical episode? No, it's not a Grey's Anatomy rerun. In plain language, you have had a medical episode when you are admitted into a hospital. If you leave and return to the hospital within 60 days for the very same reason as before, you are still having the same medical episode. You will not owe a new deductible. However, if you were admitted for a knee problem, and then you returned 60 days later for a shoulder problem, then that would be considered a new medical episode.

Part B — Doctor and Outpatient Coverage

For 2018, the Medicare Part B deductible $183 per year.[11]

Currently, after your Medicare deductible is met, you typically pay 20 percent of the Medicare-approved amount for most doctor services, (including while you are a hospital patient). That also goes for outpatient therapy and durable medical equipment. To fill in this coverage gap, many opt for additional insurance:

• Part C plans are Medicare plans administered by private insurance companies. Most Part C (Advantage Plans) come with monthly premiums, but some carriers offer them with zero premiums. It depends on where you live. It is wise to compare cost and specifics of coverage.

• Part D is a stand-alone drug plan. Premiums vary by plan and can be built into Part C plans. Again, compare costs and specifics of coverage.

---

[11] Medicare.gov. "Medicare 2018 costs at a glance."
https://www.medicare.gov/your-medicare-costs/costs-at-a-glance/costs-at-glance.html

Later in the book, we'll explore the costs and benefits of each style of plan.

Yes, according to the rules, you are covered on up to 80 percent of the medical costs, but that is for the Medicare-approved amount. For example, it does not matter what the physician or specialist charges, because Medicare has a list of reimbursements called "Diagnostic Related Groupings" (DRGs). This means that there is a master list of all the bad things that can happen to us that will require medical attention. Based on that list, Medicare will only reimburse the doctor 80 percent of the allotted amount. Remember that phrase: Medicare-approved amount.

Let's say Dorothy goes to the doctor for a condition. That doctor's normal billing schedule would charge $1,000. Since Dorothy had Medicare Part B, Medicare's DRG only allows $300 for treatment of that condition. Dorothy is only responsible for 20 percent of the $300. Dorothy is not responsible for 20 percent of the $1,000.

Sometimes the gap between what doctors actually charge and what is allowed by Medicare is substantial. The good news is that since the government controls the cost of the service, we are only responsible for 20 percent of that amount. This saved Dorothy $140.

According to the terms of the Balanced Billing Act, it is against federal law for the doctor to send a bill to the Medicare patient for the difference between what he customarily charges and the amount Medicare pays. That is why it is not too outrageous to carry only original Medicare for your health coverage when you retire, especially for those who are in very good health. I like to point out that most folks have group coverage at work before they retire that is very similar to the Medicare coverage they have after they retire. Many are like me when it comes to health insurance. If I should have to be hospitalized for something catastrophic, I have a policy with a large deductible. I also have a co-pay for doctor visits, blood work, and outpatient surgery. If that picture resembles yours, then having just plain old Medicare when you leave behind the insurance you had at work can be a parallel move.

Unlike Part A, Part B does have a monthly charge. This is a rate that is determined by the date you enroll in Part B and is means-tested. What does this mean? Depending on your income, you may have to pay more for Part B than others and recent enrollees pay a higher premium compared to the folks who have been on Part B for years. Below is a table to explain how premiums are staggered based on what we call "aging in," or, your age and income when you enrolled[12]:

Part B Premiums and Income Tax

Individual Filing	Joint Filing	Part B Premium
$85,000 to $107,000	$170,000 to $214,000	$187.50/mo
$107,000 to $133,500	$214,000 to $267,000	$267.90/mo
$133,500 to $160,000	$267,000 to $320,000	$348.30/mo
$160,000+	$320,000+	$428.60/mo

One last thing: Part B has a penalty! If you don't apply for Part B when you are first eligible and try to enroll later, you will be penalized. This does not apply to folks who choose to work beyond age 65 because they are covered by their current employer and is considered "creditable coverage." But if you do not have coverage from your current employer or the VA system and you elect not to

---

[12] Brandon, Emily. US News & World Report. March 23, 2018. "Medicare Premiums Increase for Many Beneficiaries in 2018."
https://money.usnews.com/money/retirement/medicare/articles/2018-03-23/medicare-premiums-increase-for-many-beneficiaries-in-2018

join Part B, you will be penalized in the future when you decide to join. All in all, the penalty applies to folks who decide to self-insure and then enroll in Medicare Part B later when they really need it.

Part C — Medicare Advantage

Medicare Part C (also known as MA, or Medicare Advantage) is a section of the Medicare Act created under the Medicare Modernization Act of 2003. President George W. Bush supported this sweeping change, which was the first since the original Medicare law was passed in 1965. This law created both Part C and Part D.

The basic premise of Part C, or Medicare Advantage, was to create an alternative to the original Medicare law by allowing private insurance companies to become the primary care providers and handle all billing for hospitals, doctors, and prescriptions. Ideally, it would be a streamlined billing system, where the private insurance company handles everything, and is subsidized with the Part B premium from the client. Then, the private insurance company could manage premiums all on its own with the hope that competition would curtail costs.

If you don't know whether you have Part C or not, there is a simple test. Go to your provider and show only your insurance card, not your Medicare card. If your provider accepts your insurance card only, you have Part C. If he or she requires your Medicare card and your insurance card, you do not have Part C.

There are other indicators of Part C type plans. The first is that most MA plans are network driven. That means they are a health management organization (HMO) or a preferred provider organization (PPO). You typically have lower costs when your doctor is in your network and higher costs if your doctor is out of your network. Additionally, you may not have the ability to see an out-of-network doctor without a referral.

The network-driven nature of the plans is another element of the philosophy of Part C's creation. The idea was that an individual seeing multiple doctors within the same network could avoid large emergency costs. Since one would assume the doctors in the same network are communicating with each other, they are ensuring that all preventative care is being properly managed.

Still not sure if you have a Part C plan? Medicare Advantage plans (Part C) have flat co-pays and different-sized deductibles. These are the flat amounts you pay when you visit your primary physician or specialist. Usually specialist co-pays are more than those for your primary care physician. You can always contact your insurance company to see whether you are on an advantage plan or not. To sign up for this type of plan, be sure to investigate your options and always consult a qualified and knowledgeable insurance professional.

Part D — Prescription Coverage

Medicare Part D is probably the better-known part of the Medicare Modernization Act of 2003. This is the prescription drug coverage. Since original Medicare paid nothing for prescription drugs, Medicare beneficiaries had complained for years about the high cost of medications. Health Management Organizations (HMOs) and Preferred Provider Organizations (PPOs) of the time only allowed $600 in prescription benefits per year. Over the years, the cost of prescription drugs has been rapidly rising. Some who depend on their prescription drugs to stay alive often found themselves in a position of having to decide whether to pay for food or medication. The 2003 law allowed for the creation of 45 different Medicare-approved plans that a senior could choose from to help with the costs of his or her prescriptions. Although there are limitations to what is covered and when, the amount of help for retirees went from $600 per year to $2,850 per year. This more than quadrupled the coverage.

There are four different phases — or periods — of Part D coverage:

• *Deductible period:* Until you meet your Part D deductible, you will pay the full negotiated price for your covered prescription drugs. Once you have met the deductible, the plan will begin to cover the cost of your drugs. While deductibles can vary from plan to plan, no plan's deductible can be higher than $405 in 2018, and some plans have no deductible.

• *Initial coverage period:* After you meet your deductible, your plan will help pay for your covered prescription drugs. Your plan will pay some of the cost, and you will pay a copayment or coinsurance. How long you stay in the initial coverage period depends on your drug costs and your plan's benefit structure. For most plans in 2018, the initial coverage period ends after you have accumulated $3,750 in total drug costs. (Note: Total drug costs include the amount you and your plan have paid for your covered drugs.)

• *Coverage gap:* After your total drug costs reach a certain amount ($3,750 for most plans), you enter the coverage gap, also known as the "doughnut hole." During this period, your plan does not pay for your drugs. However, as a result of health reform there are federally funded discounts that help you pay for your drugs during the doughnut hole. In 2018, there is a 65 percent discount for most brand-name drugs, paid for by the manufacturer and the federal government. This means you pay the remaining 35 percent of the cost for brand-name drugs. Similarly, the government provides a 56 percent discount for generic drugs. This means you pay the remaining 44 percent of the cost for generics.

- *Catastrophic coverage:* In all Part D plans, after you have paid $5,000 in 2018 in out-of-pocket costs for covered drugs (this amount is just the amount you have paid, not the total drug costs that you and your plan have paid), you reach catastrophic coverage. During this period, you pay significantly lower copays or coinsurance for your covered drugs for the remainder of the year. The out-of-pocket costs that help you reach catastrophic coverage include:
  - Your deductible.
  - What you paid during the initial coverage period.
  - Almost the full cost of brand-name drugs (including the manufacturer's discount) purchased during the coverage gap.
  - Amounts paid by others, including family members, most charities, and other persons on your behalf.
  - Amounts paid by State Pharmaceutical Assistance Programs (SPAPs), AIDS Drug Assistance Programs, and the Indian Health Service.[13]

Costs that do not help you reach catastrophic coverage include monthly premiums, the cost of non-covered drugs, the cost of covered drugs from pharmacies outside your plan's network, and the 49 percent generic discount. During catastrophic coverage, you will pay five percent of the cost for each of your drugs, or $3.35 for generics and $8.35 for brand-name drugs (whichever is greater).

Your Part D plan should keep track of how much money you have spent out of pocket for covered drugs and your progression through coverage periods—and this information should appear in your monthly statements.

---

[13] Medicare Interactive. "Phases of Part D Coverage." https://www.medicareinteractive.org/get-answers/medicare-prescription-drug-coverage-part-d/medicare-part-d-costs/phases-of-part-d-coverage

It is also important to know that under certain circumstances, your plan can change the cost of your drugs during the plan year. Your plan is required to alert you if such changes are made. Your plan cannot change your deductible or premium during the plan year.

Keep in mind, these four stages renew annually and are based on a calendar year.

There are many different types of plans. Some have deductibles and some do not. Some have co-pays while others have co-insurances. Some will cover generics in the coverage gap and others do not. Some have extended formularies; others stick to exactly what CMS mandates they cover. At last count, there were over 45 plans to choose from in any given area. This speaks to the variation of the Part D coverages available.

Remember, like Part B, Medicare Part D has a penalty which works in a similar way. If you are turning 65 and do not have creditable coverage through an employer or VA system, and you elect not to join Part D, you will be penalized. This penalty targets the folks who go without coverage because they are not taking medications, then decide to join later when the need to start taking medication arises.

This is basic insurance pool theory. The plan needs the healthy people, the "non-medication-taking" people, to join the pool to offset the "medication-taking" people, who will flock to join the plan as a matter of course. How do we get healthy people to join? A penalty! This is when I advise my clients to take the "avoiding penalty" plan—the lowest premium plan. It is not because they necessarily need or want the plan; it is simply to help them avoid the penalty if for any reason they need prescription drugs in the future.

Medicare Supplement and Medigap Policies

Any individual who elects not to join the Medicare Part C, or Medicare Advantage, plan is usually considering obtaining private Medicare supplement insurance. These policies are often referred to as Medigap insurance or Med Supps.

Unlike the Advantage plans, Medicare supplement plans are a secondary type of insurance that pays after Medicare pays. This means that when you go to the doctor, you will display your Medicare card and your private insurance card, or Medicare supplement card.

If Medicare approves the medical service, then the supplement plan is legally obligated to pay. If Medicare does not approve the treatment, then there is no recourse. There is no need to go to the private insurance company, because they will send you back to Medicare.

The good news with Medicare supplement plans as compared to Medicare Advantage plans is that, generally speaking, you can go to any doctor or hospital nationwide. So, you could be living in Kansas, on vacation in Florida, and go to a doctor while on vacation and still be covered. Active travelers appreciate this feature. With Medicare Advantage plans, you must stay within those networks to receive the maximum coverage and benefits. There are exceptions such as an emergency or a nationwide insurance company allowing to link in with an out-of-state network provider, but they are limited in comparison.

In some states, like my own of Massachusetts, there are only two types of Medicare supplement plans. They are named Core and Supplement 1, and the main difference (besides premium) is the coverage of the Part A deductible. Most other states have many more choices, but remember, in all states the coverage is uniform, as each carrier will have its Core and Supplement 1 plan, or their options named Plans A–J with differences in coverage and premium. If you are trying to digest the entire Medicare picture, it can be confusing. Just remember that Medicare has parts and Medicare supplement insurance has plans. Medicare's parts stop at Part D. Medicare supplement plans go all the way from Plan A to Plan J. I am told that at this writing, Plans E, H, I, and J are no longer available, but if you already have one, you can keep it.

I am not going to bore you with the details of each lettered plan. But you need to know that you have lots of options depending on your health, your income, your doctor, and where you live. For a list of different options, check out the *Medicare & You* handbook, published each year by CMS and offered in hardcopy or download from www.medicare.gov.

My goal is to educate, not confuse. Medicare has lots of moving parts, with the main ones being Parts A, B, C, and D. In the next chapter, I will take you through the four factors of Medicare planning to help shed some light on how those moving parts can be applied in your retirement plan.

CHAPTER 4

Four Factors of Medicare

"It's funny. All you have to do is say something nobody understands, and they'll do practically anything you want them to."
– J.D. Salinger

Leap years are years with 366 days, instead of the usual 365. We always tack that extra day onto February, which is the shortest month of the year and could use a little help. That creates the phenomenon of February 29 every four years.

Leap years are necessary because the actual length of a year is 365.242 days, not 365 days. By the time four years roll by, it's time to take care of that extra day. The calendar adjustment was the brainchild of Roman Emperor Julius Caesar, after whom the Julian calendar is named. Over the years it became apparent that something was off when the fall festivals on the calendar began sliding into what was clearly summertime. Caesar's attempt to fix things turned out to be a total mess, however, and the year 46 BC is still referred to as the "year of confusion." Essentially, Caesar added 99 days to the calendar that year, making it 445 days long. Calendar making was an inexact science. The best they could do was line up January 1 with the time when the day was at its shortest and start over. But the 15-month year left the people in total confusion.

My goal in all of this is not to confuse you but provide you with knowledge. But remember, these are government programs. Complexity and potential confusion are built in.

When I help my clients make up their minds regarding Medicare, there are four basic questions I ask them. These are questions you should ask yourself, too.

- What is your income?
- Who are your doctors?
- How is your health?
- Where do you live and travel?

How you answer these questions will determine which Medicare solutions are right for you. Let's take a closer look at each of these questions. You can apply your answers to each section to gain a clearer picture of what solutions you should consider. However, do not take these sections as the full deep dive into your Medicare solutions. Please be sure to discuss your options with a licensed professional.

Income

This is often the beginning of the conversation, and often the point at which it ends. Some people want to spend as much as possible on their health insurance, mainly for peace of mind. Others simply cannot. A big question is, what percentage of your income do you want to allocate toward health coverage? Spending $200 per month may not be a problem for some, while for others it may represent 20 percent of their disposable income. Only you can decide how much you wish to set aside for this purpose. But it's important to the process that you determine that number.

When you have it, write it down. We will refer to it as we move through the next three factors.

Doctors

With original Medicare and a Medicare supplement plan, you don't have to stay within a network. You just need make sure the doctor or hospital you are using accepts Medicare. Most of them do. With a Medicare Advantage plan, you will generally choose between an HMO (health maintenance organization) and a PPO (preferred provider organization). With network driven plans, it is important to find out which plans your regular physician accepts before you choose one. Unofficially, most every doctor and hospital accepts the original Medicare, but that is not always the case with Medicare Advantage plans.

If your doctor does not accept a certain plan, you must choose between your doctor and your plan. Some prefer to get the plan they prefer and find a new doctor. Decisions like this help to whittle down the options. From my perspective as a planner, making these kinds of decisions gives me a much better idea as to which plan I will recommend.

Health

Your health plays an important role in your Medicare decision. If you only go to the doctor once a year for a checkup, it is likely that you are in excellent health, so I would recommend a less expensive plan with higher co-pays for you, maybe even just original Medicare (A+B) with a stand-alone Part D plan. On the other hand, if you see the doctor often and have a chronic condition or two, I will likely recommend a more expensive plan with zero co-pays or co-pays that are as low as possible. In the long run, it will benefit you both financially and health-wise to have such a plan.

It helps to know what your total co-pays were for the previous year. This will allow us to predict what we want next year's coverage to accomplish. Assuming you do not experience a catastrophic medical expense in the next 12 months, we should be on track. If you are healthy and you continue to take good care of your health, you will reap many rewards when it comes time to choose your Medicare options. Usually these rewards are in the form of lower premiums.

Residence

CMS follows the county system. They organize the plans available in the different states according to counties. The same plan can have dramatically different premiums and levels of coverage in two counties that are side by side on the map. Two friends who live one town apart may have completely different options because of these county boundaries. This is why it is important that you deal with a Medicare professional who knows the Medicare lay of the land, so to speak, and is familiar with the plans offered in your area.

Do you travel frequently? Some Medicare Advantage plans have network restrictions, while Medicare supplement plans do not. If you travel frequently, your plan should cover you as you go. Whether your plan is limited to domestic locations or is international in scope may impact your travel plans.

The Election Periods

If it seems to you like there are a lot of choices to make when deciding on a Medicare plan, you're right! There are! Adding to that

MIND THE GAP • 43

complexity are what Medicare calls "election periods." Certain Medicare options must be chosen, or elected, at these specific times of the year and no other.

IEP — Initial Election Period

The first election period is wrapped around the month you turn age 65. It actually begins three months before you turn 65, and then extends three months after you turn 65, and then there's the month in which you turn 65. It is the seven-month period of time you are given to decide whether you wish to be enrolled in Medicare Part B. You will automatically be enrolled in Medicare Part A as soon as you turn 65. Remember, Part B is the portion of your coverage that comes with a premium and covers doctor visits. Part A covers "medical episodes" in the hospital.

If you continue to work, you can elect to enroll in Part B when you retire or lose the insurance coverage you had through your employer. You could also elect to go ahead and get your Part B while you are still working. This is a decision you will need to weigh out with your trusted advisor.

AEP — The Fall Election Period

Now, if you chose to continue working, or for any other reason did not enroll in Part B during your IEP, you may do so during the AEP (Annual Election Period). AEP runs from October 17 through December 7 each year and gives you the opportunity to change your Medicare Advantage plan, Medicare supplement plan, or Part D plan.

Logically, this is the time to look at your coverage and where we apply our four factors and see which of the plans is most suitable for you. You may elect to change your plan or leave it the way it is. If it is in your best interest to change your plan, this is the time to do it. Evaluate your options and decide what makes the best sense for you.

Medicare Advantage Disenrollment Period –
The Winter Election Period

Think of this as your "regret" enrollment period. It runs from January 1 to February 14 of each year. If you signed up for a Part C plan but then realized that none of your doctors are in the plan and you want to change back to original Medicare, then pick up a Medicare Supplement. Please note there are some changes that are allowed during this period but not all changes are allowed. The AEP is the best and most flexible time for Medicare insurance analysis.

SEP - Special Election Periods and 5-Star Enrollment Periods

There are many other instances where people can make elections throughout the year due to losing creditable coverage, moving to a new area or enrolling in a 5-Star plan which is a highly rated plan and is granted additional enrollments. Be aware that these are available and need to be utilized so you don't have a gap in coverage.

Conclusion

Although very expensive to our country, Medicare is a great tool for retirement. People can see their health insurance costs plummet from $1,000 per month to $150 per month, especially if they are paying their own premiums. In many cases, health insurance costs prevent individuals from taking early retirement. The would-be retiree must wait until he or she turns 65, when Medicare kicks in, and then try to pick up some type of supplemental insurance. Now, with those savings, retirement becomes a possibility where it was not one before.

Since there is a gap in the coverage from original Medicare, you will want to carefully weigh the four factors mentioned here as you decide how much you wish to invest toward your premium. Make sure you know the gaps in coverage, the $1,340 deductible (as of

2018) for Part A and the 20 percent for Part B. Then ask yourself the key questions about your income, your doctors, your health, and your place of residence when making your Medicare plans. Don't miss out on your election periods. At the very least, the AEP in your area is a great time to review your plans and make adjustments where needed. You will find the right balance to filling in your health insurance gaps that will be waiting for you at age 65.

A few years ago, when some of these programs were undergoing so many changes, I tuned into a radio talk station driving home from work. On the line was a caller who was expressing frustration at the many moving parts of the government-run health care system.

"I'm an attorney with a both a law degree and a doctorate in finance," he said, "and I have read every paragraph in the guidelines and I still can't make heads or tails of it."

I sympathize with the attorney. Understanding Medicare and Medicaid, and all the cousin programs that go with them, can present a challenge. Then, once you understand it, you must keep an attentive eye and ear for the minor changes in the regulations that take place over time. But much can be gained by understanding all your options and making informed choices. I have seen poor choices cost individuals thousands of dollars each year. What a needless loss. And Uncle Sam will never send you a letter telling you what to do. Nor will you get a postcard from your senator or congressman telling you that your choice didn't match your circumstances. It's your responsibility to pick the right plan. I will say it one more time: when in doubt, seek professional guidance from a licensed advisor.

CHAPTER 5

Bridging the Gaps in Long-Term Care

"I may not have gone where I intended to go, but I think I have ended up where I needed to be."
– Douglas Adams, Author, "The Hitchhiker's Guide to the Galaxy"

Over the years, I must have had the same conversation with hundreds of families, and it is never a pleasant subject to discuss. What would happen if you went into a nursing home?

Some aspects of aging we look forward to, such as the free time after retirement to pursue a hobby like painting and writing or playing with our grandchildren. Whatever your dream may be, what is most important is that you have one. But no one I know of likes to think about the possibility of being confined to a long-term care facility. In fact, most people think it will never happen to them. As uncomfortable as the subject is, we have to talk about it, folks, because, according to the financial research firm The Motley Fool, most of us will need some form of long-term care during our lifetimes.[14]

Most people end up paying for nursing home care out of their savings until they run out of money, then they can qualify for Medicaid to pick up the cost. The advantages of paying privately are that you are more likely to gain entrance to a better facility and doing so eliminates or postpones dealing with your state's welfare bureaucracy — an often demeaning and time-consuming process. The disadvantage is that it's expensive.

Careful planning can save you money and grief down the road. Naturally, the best planning is that which is done in advance of a situation. But even planning in response to an unanticipated need for care can help protect your estate. One way to plan for this rainiest of days is to buy long-term care insurance while others consider the more novel hybrid solutions that have been gaining traction; both of which we will discuss in detail in subsequent chapters of this book.

Failing to Plan is Planning to Fail

Does ignoring the likelihood of an unpleasant development and failing to plan for it prevent it from happening? Nope. Of course, you know where I stand on this, because planning is part of my job description. It is my professional "middle name," so to speak. Planning is doing the research on behalf of my clients, presenting all options, and helping the clients make a well-informed decision. Regardless of the challenge, the process is the same. However, you are the one who ultimately must decide whether you will address

---

[14] Campbell, Todd. The Motley Fool. June 10, 2017. "Your 2017 Guide to Long-Term Care and Long-Term Care Insurance."
https://www.fool.com/investing/general/2017/06/10/your-2017-guide-to-long-term-care-and-long-term-ca.aspx

the issue while you are relatively young and healthy, or just let it slide. The latter is not recommended. It's called "managing by emergency," and it seldom has a happy ending. Frankly, it is the government making decisions for you rather than you controlling your own destiny. Which would you prefer?

I love what hiking does for the spirit. Getting away occasionally from telephones and the noisy bustle of the workaday world is a psychological tonic for me. Two or three days on the trail is just the brain massage I need sometimes to keep the mental edge required by my regular job, which is dragon slaying and damsel rescuing (financially speaking, of course). Trail hiking, or backpacking, as some refer to it, requires special planning. If you are going away for a weekend and everything you will eat and use for sleeping is on your back, it requires a bit of thought and preparation. The backpack can't be too heavy, or it makes getting from point A to point B virtually impossible. So that eliminates a lot of canned foods or frozen meats and superfluous equipment. But the backpack can't be too light, either. Some things are absolute necessities on the trail and you won't succeed without them. After you have packed your water filter, plus your dehydrated and freeze-dried food items, which are lightweight and easy to carry, you must still have room for a tent, sleeping bag and cooking utensils.

Like many things in life, you can both seek and follow the advice of those who know, or just wing it and learn the hard way. I much prefer the former. It saves considerable time. Before my first wilderness hiking experience, I consulted with the professionals at the outdoors shop where I was to purchase some of my gear. Down-filled, zero-degree sleeping bag — check. Portable, folding propane stove and fuel tank — check. Waterproof matches — check. Extra plastic water bottle — check. The list went on. The professionals who had blazed the trails before me told me I would need all this stuff, and they were right. My pack weighed 42 pounds, a little more than I wanted, but I was pleased and eager to go.

Because I had planned ahead, I had a pleasant experience on the trail. I wish I could say the same about one of the other hikers in our party. His pack was thrown together at the last minute and he had a miserable time. He saw no need for the small but sturdy nylon tent. He thought why not just sleep out under the stars, since there was no rain in the forecast. Since we were all novices, no one among us could give our fellow hiker a good reason why that wasn't OK. He found out the next morning, however, when he discovered that the dew, which settles on everything during the night, had completely saturated his sleeping bag, rendering it useless as protection from the chilly night air.

Winston Churchill said, "Failing to plan is planning to fail," an axiom that certainly applies to our financial lives, especially when health care is concerned. On the face of things, when it comes to health care, planning is simple — do it and do it early. If that is the case, then why do so many people fail to plan for the eventuality of needing skilled nursing care at some point in their lives by not planning for it? The answer is (a) denial, it'll never happen to me, (b) because it costs too much, (c) it is difficult to understand, or (d) most importantly, they are unaware of all the new modern techniques for LTC planning.

Before we get into what long-term care planning is and is not, and what it does and does not do, let's first consider what Medicare does and does not do, because some are under the mistaken impression that Medicare covers long-term care.

The Gap

The gap between what Medicare covers and the actual need isn't just a gap — it's a yawning chasm. Technically, Medicare will pay for 100 days in a nursing home, and the rough equivalent for home health care. But to understand where Medicare truly ends, you need to read the fine print. Medicare will pay for that time if, and only if, you are receiving what is considered skilled care. "Skilled care" is defined as around-the-clock, 24-hour-a-day nursing care necessary for the patient so that he or she can continue to improve. This "improvement" is the key to understanding whether you will receive the 100 days or not.

Let's say you are going through rehabilitation, recovering from surgery, or a fall, or a lengthy stay in the hospital. Medicare will pay and cover the costs for 100 days if you're continuing to get better. But the minute the doctors consider you to have reached a plateau in your recovery, whether it is in 20 days or 30 days, Medicare pulls the plug. Think of it as a discharge from the hospital. You are covered while in the hospital by Medicare Part A, as we have learned. When you are sent over to a rehabilitation center, Medicare Part A will continue to cover that expense — because that is considered skilled care — and will continue to do so for the next 100 days. But then, if you are discharged from rehabilitation because you are deemed to have "plateaued" (you are no longer improving), the skilled care ends and with it goes Medicare... even if you only change floors in the same building. Welcome to the gap!

This can be an inconvenience if you are relatively healthy. But if you are elderly, and you fall and break a hip, and you hit that plateau, being in the gap can have some unfavorable consequences. You are still unable to get around and fend for yourself and you still need medical attention, but it doesn't matter. Medicare will not pay. If you don't have private insurance to take over, go ahead and get your checkbook out. You will be paying $4,000–$12,000 per month for what is considered long-term care.

The same rules apply to home health care as to rehabilitation. Medicare will cover home health care for skilled nursing care and physical therapy until you stop improving. Once you hit the improvement plateau — and this is the doctor's call — Medicare ends, and you are responsible for the bill. Discussing this over coffee one afternoon with a representative of these government programs, he said, "Matt, we only have so many resources to go around and we have to limit what we pay for. If it is an open-ended situation, like long-term care, Medicare simply can't cover all of those costs. That's what Medicaid does."

Medicaid Planning

"But you have to be deemed penniless to get Medicaid, don't you?" I asked. He just rolled his eyes. From what this man said, and from what I researched, Medicaid spends two-thirds of its annual budget on the disabled and those who are older than 65 in long-term care facilities, even though it was designed to provide health insurance for low-income people and those on welfare. According to the Kaiser Commission on Medicaid and the Uninsured, Medicaid picks up the tab for most of the 1.7 million Americans who occupy nursing home beds. One report puts the average cost for nursing home stays at $85,775 per year for a semiprivate room and $97,455 per year for a private room. The average cost of home health services is $47,934 per year, and $45,000 per year for assisted living facilities.[15]

The Kaiser Foundation also reports that Medicaid covers six out of 10 people living in nursing homes. Many of these people are middle-class individuals who, having burned through their savings, are as dependent upon the program as people who never had the money in the first place. While the program was intended for only low-income people, many individuals who live comfortable lives, own property, and have substantial home equity choose to adjust their net worth to fit the government's definition of "low income" and thus qualify for Medicaid if they enter a nursing home.

---

[15] Genworth, 2017. "Compare Long Term Care Costs Across the United States." https://www.genworth.com/aging-and-you/finances/cost-of-care.html

They must do this financial maneuvering five years before the need arises, however, because they are subject to a five-year look back. The purpose of this is to prevent those above the eligibility levels for Medicaid from giving away their resources at the last minute just so they can qualify for nursing home care under Medicaid.[16]

During the look-back period, the state can open your books to see if you have transferred anything out of your name. This includes gifts to grandchildren, gifts to children to purchase homes, help toward college education, property transfers, etc. The auditors are looking for anything of value that you gave away to anybody and for which you were not paid a fair market value in return.

The auditors count everything, too. Even that $15,000 (the annual IRS gift exclusion for 2018) chunk of your grandchildren's inheritance that you gave to them so you could see them enjoy it during their lifetime is counted. You may have received repayment in the form of love and gratitude, but unless they gave you something of $15,000 provable value in return, in the state's eyes that is a disqualifying transfer. For Medicaid qualification purposes, the $15,000 bounces right back into your name. I know of one couple whose resources allowed them to give $15,000 to each of their nine grandchildren. That's a $135,000 bounce-back! The same goes for cash, stocks, bonds, property — anything that was given away within five years of an application to Medicaid. It must be accounted for.

The Deficit Reduction Act of 2005 (DRA) drastically changed the qualifications for nursing home care via Medicaid, making them much stricter. If advance preparations aren't made for a loved one's care, most, if not all, of an estate — the entire fruits of a

---

[16] Henry J. Kaiser Family Foundation. June 20, 2017. "Medicaid's Role in Nursing Home Care." https://www.kff.org/infographic/medicaids-role-in-nursing-home-care

hardworking American's lifetime of labor — can vanish. That is why modern Medicaid Planning began in 2006. From that point on, if you were doing an irrevocable trust, you would be OK in five years. If you were doing a life estate on your primary residence, you would be OK in five years. If you gave those gifts to grandchildren, you would be OK in five years. Before the DRA became law, the look-back period was three years.

At first glance, the changes in the Deficit Reduction Act may seem harsh; yet in many ways they help protect the general taxpayer. If Medicaid were easier to qualify for, it would impose a greater burden on the taxpayers. After the party, someone has to pick up the tab. But some of the regulations can cause pain. One example is the new regulations pertaining to penalty periods. The penalty period is how long you are ineligible for Medicaid if they see that you have made gifts of your money within the look-back period.

Prior to the DRA, the transfer penalty period began the month after the transfer was made. For example, on the old system, if you had transferred $100,000 to your children, the state would divide that amount by the monthly cost of a nursing home and determine a monthly penalty period that you could not receive state aid.

Example: $100,000 divided by $6,000 equals 16.6 months.

Before DRA, if 16.6 months had elapsed since you transferred that $100,000, you would be OK even if it was within the five years. This is no longer the case.

Under DRA the transfer begins the month a person is institutionalized and otherwise eligible for Medicaid. Now, auditors assess the 16.6 months from the date you apply for state aid. If you transferred $100,000 at any point in the five years, you would be ineligible for benefits for 16.6 months from the date you applied for care. If you tried to get Medicaid benefits, they would say, "Yes, we'll help, but only after a year and four months have passed. Talk to us next year, and if you still need help, we will see what we can do."

In my view, it is not unethical for senior citizens who are caught between the "rock" of rising long-term care costs and the "hard place" of dwindling resources to try to fit into the Medicaid qualifications window. I am not saying that those who are truly wealthy should use it as a means to become wealthier still. I doubt that would be the case anyway. The quality of care paid for by Medicaid is not necessarily subpar, all things considered, but it is hardly the luxury that the truly wealthy can afford. If Medicaid solves a problem for hurting Americans, and it doesn't break the law, then there is no foul. It bridges the gap left by Medicare and private health insurance plans. How ironic it is that many seniors are considered too "rich" to receive Medicaid, but if they go into a nursing home they'll soon see most of their assets disappear.

The government uses the term "spend down" in their official literature to describe the process by which a potential Medicaid applicant will spend down his resources to qualify. The regulations provide a menu for such spending. Money spent on items on the menu is not subject to the look-back process. These expenditures may include:

- Prepaying funeral expenses
- Paying off a mortgage
- Making repairs to a home
- Replacing an old automobile
- Updating home furnishings
- Paying for more care at home
- Even buying a new home

That is a simplified list. There are details you will want to examine closely with the help of a professional or elder law attorney before making major decisions. In the case of married couples, for example, it's important that any spend-down steps be taken only after the unhealthy spouse moves to a nursing home if this would affect the community spouse's resource allowance. "Community spouse" is Medicaid lingo for the husband or wife of a Medicaid applicant. To qualify as a community spouse, you must be the husband or wife of an "institutionalized spouse," meaning a person who resides in a medical institution or nursing facility and is "likely to remain there for at least 30 consecutive days."

Here's a sampling of what long-term health care costs in America these days.

2017 National Health Care Costs[17]

Type	Average Daily Rate	Average Annual Rate
Nursing Home (Private Room)	$267	$97,455
Nursing Home (Semi-Private Room)	$235	$85,775
Assisted Living	$123	$45,000
Home Health Care	$135	$49,192
Adult Day Care	$70	$18,200

The sheer cost of long-term care is what always struck me. At this writing, it has been 17 years since I first entered the financial planning profession, and I was stunned to find out how much elder care costs and the harsh nature of the trap that is lying in wait for millions of Americans who do not plan. All across this great land of ours, there are hardworking people who are making all the right decisions. They are saving. They are putting their children through college. They are socking money away into their IRAs and 401(k)s. They are establishing wills and estate plans. And then, at the very end of their lives, something happens and "poof"—all of those years

---

[17] Genworth Financial. June 2017. 2017 Genworth Cost of Care Report. https://www.genworth.com/aging-and-you/finances/cost-of-care.html.

of hard work and good decision making vanishes like dandelion snow in a wind gust.

All in all, it is good to know that we do have a safety net that catches us if we do not plan, but let's not put lipstick on a pig: Medicaid is welfare.

Most folks I know work as hard as they can not to be on welfare. They look at it like being on the state's dole. When you are on Medicaid, you are a ward of the state, and they have all the say in where and how you receive care. Because they are paying the bill, they make the rules.

Medicaid Trusts and Medicaid Annuities

I don't believe in self-dentistry. It isn't prudent, and it sounds painful. I am also a big advocate of seeing a doctor when you are seriously ill, and not asking your neighbor to perform a little surgery on you next Saturday afternoon. I always cringe when I hear the expression "self-medication." It sounds dangerous and it usually is. Speaking to a professional about long-term care planning, especially when it may involve Medicare and Medicaid, is always a good idea. There are people out there whose chosen career is to know all the wrinkles of those programs. They are fully trained in planning for health care costs, and they keep their ear to the ground for the slightest changes in the programs that are available for senior citizens. They are experienced in providing options and strategies that (and I mean no disrespect here) you probably don't even know exist.

For decades now, some attorneys who specialize in law for elder care have incorporated Medicaid planning into their client services. There are several reasons why consulting with an attorney who specializes in elder issues is a wise move.

(1) Every state's Medicaid system is different. The state's Medicaid system is funded 50/50 — 50 percent comes from the states and 50 percent from the federal government. Guidelines are issued from the federal level, but leeway is given to the state. For help understanding your state's labyrinthine laws, contact an attorney who understands issues for the elderly, and the laws applicable in your state.

(2) There are safe harbors available for certain property and assets, such as final expenses, personal vehicles, income-generating property, benefits to family members who assist with care, and many others. The attorney who specializes in law for the elderly is to know where these safe harbors are and how they work.

These attorneys are in the best position to tell you what trusts would be in your best interests to have drawn up. The paperwork for these must be done correctly. Otherwise, they are invalidated when the time comes to execute them. Trusts can be tedious to prepare, but your local professional has likely prepared hundreds of them and can assist you.

The Usefulness of Trusts

The problem with transferring assets is that you have given them away. You no longer control them, and even a trusted child or other relative may lose them. A safer approach is to put them in an irrevocable trust. A trust is a legal entity under which one person — the trustee — holds legal title to property for the benefit of others who are beneficiaries. The trustee must follow the rules provided in the trust instrument. Whether trust assets are counted against Medicaid's resource limits depends on the terms of the trust and who created it. A "revocable" trust is one that may be changed or rescinded by the person who created it. Medicaid considers the principal of such trusts (that is, the funds that make up the trust) to be assets that are countable in determining Medicaid eligibility. When people ask me about trusts and whether they are protected from spend down, I always tell them that the key is understanding the difference between revocable trusts and irrevocable trusts. If you can revoke a trust, that means you still have control over the assets. Irrevocable trusts, as the term implies, are set in stone. Is the trust one that you still control, or is it one that is not controlled by you? For the purposes of Medicaid planning, only irrevocable trusts are viable as possible safe havens from spend down. Assets contained in a trust over which you have control are still in your possession.

When it comes to trusts and other legal ways to transfer assets, remember that the five-year look-back period still applies. Whether you are transferring assets out of your control by gifting or putting a child's name on the deed to a piece of property, or whether you are assigning ownership to the trust, the five-year look-back period is in effect. If you still control the asset, even if it is in a trust, then Medicaid can insist that you spend down those assets before you are deemed eligible for the program. What if the assets were in a revocable trust for 20 years or more? It doesn't matter. In their eyes, if you still control the trust, then you can access the assets inside to pay for care.

A word of caution. The use of a trust may cause Medicaid to scrutinize all transfers more closely. For example, transfer of a residence into a trust with the elderly person retaining the right to live in the house may cause the Department of Job and Family Services (the agency that manages the Medicaid program) to argue that the person has retained an interest in the home sufficient to disqualify him from Medicaid benefits. You may be able to counter that by leasing the property. But the paperwork must be correctly filled out, and if the grantor or spouse remains in the home, he or she must make payments at the fair rental value of the property. The Internal Revenue Code complicates the drafting of these trusts, so seeking professional advice from an attorney specializing in laws for the elderly will save you lots of grief down the road. The attorney will be able to acquaint you with such things as:

- Tax consequences of transfers
- Exempt transfers
- Income only trusts
- Testamentary trusts
- Supplemental needs trusts
- Life estates

What about Medicaid Annuities?

In some cases, liquid assets can be converted into an income stream using an annuity. However, it can't be just any type of annuity; it must be a Medicaid qualified annuity. Keeping track of the various state and federal rules governing Medicaid is like trying to herd cats: About the time you think you know all the little nuances of the system, up pops a new one. Keep your eye on each provision that makes it possible to have your cake and eat it, too. It will likely hide where you can't find it.

In most states, for an immediate annuity to be considered an exempt asset for Medicaid, it generally must meet these conditions:

- It must be **irrevocable** and **non-assignable**. This means it can't be redeemed or sold. That means that all deferred annuities are countable by Medicaid. They won't help you qualify.
- It must be **actuarially sound**, which means that the annuity must be designed to pay off the entire asset value over the actual, or expected, annuitant's lifetime. In theory, the annuity has to pay you back the entire purchase cost within the life expectancy as set forth in Medicaid tables. You can't use mortality tables used for tax purposes or those published by insurance companies.

Another word of caution. Each state has its own rules about these annuities. Some states, like California, don't even like to hear the terms "Medicaid annuities" or Medicaid-qualified annuities" used. It's important to use the services of a financial professional who specializes in insurance products for senior citizens to make sure you have a "map to the minefield," so to speak.

Conclusion

Although we should all feel at ease knowing that there is a safety net that will catch us and not put us out on the street in the event of a chronic illness, it is not exactly a smooth landing, nor should it be. Having to spend down your assets at a very high rate is extremely burdensome on top of the emotional fallout of being in a nursing home or having to put a loved one in a nursing home. Certainly, the facilities do all they can to make us feel at home and as welcome as possible, but we all know that it is not the same. And certainly, attorneys and financial planners like me do last-minute planning with folks with Medicaid annuities or the use of irrevocable trusts in the comprehensive plan. But this is by far the most difficult gap to bridge in retirement due to the costs and requires the most extensive planning. Let's explore the more favorable options in the next chapter and let the reader take the next step.

CHAPTER 6

Long-Term Care Planning: Things You Need to Know

"Fun is like life insurance; the older you get, the more it costs."
– Kin Hubbard, American humorist

If an insurance professional was to have fallen asleep 20 years ago, like the famed fictional character Rip Van Winkle, and awakened today, he wouldn't recognize the business. There have been so many changes in the world of insurance that someone should think up a new name for it. Of course, the basic idea is still the same — spreading the risk to absorb the cost. The concept of insurance began in 100 BC when a Roman army officer by the name of Caius Marius started a "burial club" for his troops. As members of the club, soldiers would contribute financially to the club to cover the cost of their burial. The Romans believed that if you didn't want to have a tortured afterlife, your family must have an elaborate ceremony to honor you when you die. This spreading of the risk funded many a "proper burial" in ancient Rome. The idea caught on. Burial clubs were formed in other regiments. Roman soldiers were the best in the world. While taking on the Huns and the

Barbarians was a risky business, more soldiers made it back alive than died in battle. Soon there was enough money in the club's account to not only bury the unfortunate soldiers who didn't make it through a battle, but to pay their widow and families a healthy stipend as well.

Eventually, these burial clubs became popular with common citizens. After all, no one wanted a tortured spirit in the afterlife. After the fall of Rome in 476 AD, the burial clubs disappeared. The idea was reborn as life insurance in 1662 when Englishman John Graunt created the first life expectancy tables. He researched statistics until he could predict, with reasonable accuracy, how long an average individual would live, based on his or her age, health and other factors. Now that human mortality could be calculated, and mortality could be predicted to a reasonable degree, companies began springing up to offer contracts to individuals that followed the same concept established by the old Roman burial clubs. By the 18th century, it was common to find underwriters, as these first insurance professionals were called, meeting in cafes, discussing the risks and investments on the policies. They were called "underwriters" because it was their name at the bottom of the contract. That signature indicated they would make good on the promises within the policy, come what may. Europe had, after all, experienced epidemics where hundreds of thousands had died of disease. These underwriters were placing their fortunes at risk in hopes of making a profit. Modern life insurance, with underwriters, risk, mortality tables, policies, premiums, government regulation and representative agents, would appear some time later.

In the United States, in 1759, the Presbyterian Church sponsored an early form of insurance — a fund to benefit their ministers. Soon, other religious organizations followed suit. It didn't take long for the concept to attract the attention of businessmen. In a 50-year period, from 1787 to 1837, more than 20 profit-based insurance companies appeared.

Traditional LTC Insurance Appears

Over the centuries, insurance of all kinds appeared on the scene. These days, you can insure anything from boats to baboons. It wasn't until the 1970s that the concept of long-term care insurance was created. Before then, families didn't see the need for such protection. There were few nursing homes. Most families took care of their aging relatives at home, often without adequate medical care. Following World War II, stay-at-home caregivers were becoming a disappearing breed. Once again, just as it was the case in ancient Rome, a need was created that insurance could fill. Like nature, the free enterprise system abhors a vacuum, so the need was filled by the introduction of LTC policies.

Many of the nursing homes that existed prior to the 1970s offered less than standard care, so regulation and standardization came along to make insurance policies easier for companies to underwrite. Medicare and private health insurance would pay only for a limited amount of time if a patient was discharged from a hospital but still needed skilled nursing care. Instead of a payment for services rendered, Medicare paid a lump sum based on a predetermined amount for a specific illness. Medicare paid for 21 days in the nursing home, the amount extended to 100 days when you had a supplement, and the rest was the responsibility of the patient. Medicare and the supplement paid nothing if skilled care was not needed.

Hospitals were discharging their patients sooner once Medicare changed its reimbursement rules. Many of the elderly in nursing homes didn't exactly need skilled nursing care as much as they needed help dressing themselves or performing the normal activities of daily living. To address these issues and offer policies to cover the various levels of care needed, they used activities of daily living (ADLs) as a baseline to define qualification for such care. These activities included bathing, dressing, eating, toileting, transferring from bed to chair and maintaining continence. As the competition for business grew, insurance companies lowered the number of activities necessary to qualify for payment.

Insurance, like everything else in the world, evolves and changes in response to the environment in which it exists and the purpose it serves. LTC insurance soon expanded to accommodate a growing desire and need for home health care. The coverage was either a stand-alone home health care policy or a rider on a nursing home policy. Normally the payment was half the daily amount selected for nursing homes if it was part of a long-term care nursing home policy. Eventually, policies offered payment for assisted care, adult day care, homemaker's services, personal care, home health care, hospice care and even respite care for a family member taking care of the elderly person.

How LTC Insurance Works

Compared to traditional life insurance, traditional long-term care insurance is young, but it follows the same model as term life insurance. Your premium is determined by age and health. You pay as little as possible so that, in the event you use a nursing home or home health care later in life, you will be indemnified from the cost of such care. What happens if you "die with your boots on," so to speak, and don't ever need long-term care? The premiums you paid go into the insurance pool to pay for others who do need the care. That may seem unfair, but the reverse could be the case, too. You could pay only one month's worth of premiums and suffer a health catastrophe that would land you in a nursing home for years. In that case the policy would cover you for hundreds of thousands of dollars. To encourage people to purchase long-term care policies, the federal government allowed a tax deduction for premiums starting in 1997. Some state governments instituted partnership programs. If you purchase a partnership plan and outlive the benefits, the state pays for the balance of your stay at the nursing home, or at home health care, thus protecting your personal assets. Other states, like Massachusetts and Wisconsin, instituted an exemption on the client's primary residence as an incentive program for people to own traditional long-term care insurance. Remember, this is not a gift to the insurance industry; rather, it is the government's way of shifting the burden of long-term care from the taxpayer (Medicaid) to the insurer.

Typically, these plans are comprehensive in the sense that they cover nursing home care, home health care, and assisted living facilities. To reduce costs, however, you can opt for a "facility only" plan.

There are other options to modify the premium. For example, you can modify the deductible (elimination period), decide whether to adjust for inflation, add a survivorship benefit, or add a waiver of premium. The myriad of choices that allow you to fine tune these plans goes on and on. Think of an ice cream sundae buffet. You start with a bare vanilla scoop and add toppings as you wish, upping the cost with each topping.

Cost Is the Biggest Objection: For Us & Them

The cost of traditional LTC insurance is expensive. According to the American Association for Long-Term Care Insurance, a couple, age 60, will pay $3,490 per year for an initial pool of benefits of $164,000 for each spouse with a 3 percent rise in benefits annually. But here's the kicker. You may need to spend twice as much to be adequately covered. As has already been pointed out, the national average cost for a private nursing home room is more than $267 per day, or $97,455 per year.[18]

Another drawback is your premium is not locked in. If you want to keep the coverage from lapsing, you must pay the rate increases that occur frequently, or buy a special rider when you buy the policy that locks in the premium. Can your insurance company raise your premiums because your health changes once you are on the books? No. Can they change your premium because you are getting older as time goes by? No. But they can raise premiums for broad classes of policyholders when their profit picture darkens. Recent history has not been kind to the long-term care insurance industry and should put you on heightened alert if exploring this option. Basically, the policies were mispriced to begin with, working under the assumption that the insurance pool would grow with new policyholders; yet when the first claims begin to pile up and enrollment didn't increase, the insurance companies were forced to increase premiums. What is worse, many insurance companies are exiting the business. When I began in the field in 2001, there were many companies offering long-term care insurance, and now you can count them on one hand. I advise you to check with your LTC planner to make sure that the company you are selecting has an overall good reputation and a positive stature when it comes to paying claims and keeping premiums stable.

The way I look at it, when you get hit by a rate increase, you can do one of three things: (a) bite the bullet and pay the higher premiums to keep your policy in force, (b) scale back on your coverage and reduce your cost, or (c) drop your policy. My advice is to hold on to your existing policy if you can afford to do so. I think it's better to reduce coverage than to drop it altogether. Only the

---

[18] American Association for Long-Term Care Insurance. "2018 National Long-Term Care Insurance Price Index." http://www.aaltci.org/news/wp-content/uploads/2018/01/2018-Price-Index-LTC.pdf

insurance company benefits when you drop a policy that you have paid into for several years.

If the higher premiums are just too much, however, you can lower your premiums by adjusting the benefit period from five years to, say, three years. The average claim for LTC insurance is less than three years. You can also lower your daily benefit or extend the waiting period. You could change the inflation protection, but I would put that last on the list.

A "Use It or Lose It" Proposition

Until recently, LTC was dominated by the traditional policies for decades, the terms of which were essentially a "use it or lose it" proposition. If you didn't use the benefits, then the premiums would go to the insurance company and be used to pay benefits to other folks who used long-term care services. If you stop and think about it, that's the way insurance works. Large numbers spread the risk.

Traditional long-term care is still available, and the concept is viable. But the ultimate test of viability of any product is how the public receives it, and the public wasn't too keen on traditional LTC insurance. For the most part, the average consumer is still shying away from it and this is not being helped with the recent increase in premiums.

The idea of spending as much as $50,000 in insurance premiums over your lifetime and having nothing to leave as a legacy for your heirs is a bit distasteful. This is one of the reasons why the hybrid products are becoming more popular. They scratch an itch. But the insurance industry has done a poor job of letting people know that these alternative approaches to LTC insurance exist. Before we explore the other planning alternatives, let's discuss what long-term care covers and what needs to be addressed.

The Face of Long-Term Care

The mention of long-term care usually conjures up the mental picture of a nursing home. That is not always reality, however. LTC includes three general areas and variations and combinations in between. Any planning session needs to take these three areas into account. In the future we are likely to see even more alternative care options, such as expanded adult day care and continuing care retirement communities. For now, let's stick with the basics.

Nursing home care: This is defined as "around-the-clock" care, but not necessarily skilled care, which is the biggest difference between rehabilitation facilities and nursing homes. What confuses some is that most hospitals will have both a rehabilitation wing and a skilled nursing care wing. Call it a nursing home wing, for all practical purposes. You may be in the same building, but your level of care is different. From a planning perspective, that means there is a difference between which one is covered by insurance and which is not. As we will see, Medicare and traditional health insurances cover rehab stays because rehab is considered a temporary stay of intensive care. However, a nursing home stay is considered to be chronic and open-ended. Here's another gap to consider when discussing coverage. Since nursing home care is not covered by traditional insurance, long-term care planning will address this gap in coverage.

The insurance industry and care facilities work with a standard when it comes to who can be admitted to a nursing home and qualify for benefits. Typically – and there are exceptions – this standard requires that the patient be unable to perform two out of six of what are referred to as activities of daily living (ADLs) mentioned earlier in this chapter: bathing, dressing, eating, toileting, transferring from bed to chair, and maintaining continence. Cognitive impairment is another condition that makes one eligible to receive LTC benefits. An example of cognitive impairment is Alzheimer's disease, or other forms of dementia, such as the more uncommon Pick's disease. If you are familiar with the effects of dementia, you know that there are stages involved, and evaluation is necessary before benefits can come into play. The emotional and financial challenges that accompany these disorders are formidable and life-changing.

Assisted living: Assisted living facilities have grown in popularity in the past 20 years. They can be found throughout the country, offering varying degrees of care. In general terms, assisted living facilities are viewed as places that facilitate semi-independent living. Nurses are on staff for emergencies, but it is expected that residents can perform for themselves the six normal activities of daily living mentioned earlier. It is often a midway point for those who can fend for themselves without assistance but do need a measure of medical attention.

Once an individual is medically deemed no longer able to perform the normal activities of daily living, he or she is typically relocated to a nursing home, since the assisted living facility would be underqualified to care for him or her.

The cost of assisted living facilities varies by accommodations and location, just like the cost of nursing home care and home health care. Assisted living facilities are not covered at all by traditional health insurance. But the good news is that, with long-term care planning, you can use the proceeds to cover the monthly cost of an assisted living facility. Of course, to qualify for the insurance benefits, the care and the coverage parameters must match up, and your evaluation by a qualified medical professional must match the terms of the policy. On the other hand, for families that are using self-insurance methods, these limitations do not exist.

Home health care: This is by far the most preferable form of care, since it combines the care that you would receive at a rehab facility, a nursing home, and an assisted living facility, but all within the confines of your own home. Why doesn't everyone go that route? It's not that easy to qualify for. Home health care requires coordination and coverage, meaning that to establish a solid home health care plan, you need a care coordinator who manages the nurses, the therapists, aides, and any other professionals who may be needed to administer the care. But from a planning perspective, it can be done. One strategy involves planning for the care in layers, depending on how advanced the illness or incapacitation is. Medicare will pay for some home health care, according to the same rules that apply to care in a rehabilitation facility. You must be getting better or become in need of skilled health care to get you back on your feet. If that is your case, then you are covered. If it is not, the benefits stop.

Like rehab, the coverage for home health care is limited. You may need intermediate care, such as help bathing and dressing, or just running errands to keep the house in good order. This is called "custodial" care by some plans, and coverage will sometimes fund a "care management coordinator" to further facilitate the stay at home. Coverage for this can be included in long-term care planning.

Why Long-Term Care and Comprehensive Planners Exist

If you are thinking that all of this is a little complex, you are not alone. Have you ever stepped inside the cockpit of a passenger jetliner? I did, back before the days of terrorism and Homeland Security, when all you had to do was be nice to the pilots and they would give you a tour. Did you see all the dials and switches and computer displays? Intimidating, wasn't it? But to a trained pilot, it is no more confusing than the keys of a piano are to a pianist, or the valves on a saxophone are to a jazz musician. Once you understand it, LTC planning can be tweaked and adjusted to fit the care. That's why long-term care and comprehensive financial planners exist.

They are trained to know all the ins and outs of the care, the facilities that render it, the policies that cover it, and the necessary team members to organize it. They are fully trained to know how to match up the care with the coverage, and, of course, stay within the budget. Choosing options can be made simple once you understand what is likely, what is unlikely, and where the coverage lines are among Medicare, Medicaid, private insurance, and self-funding.

One More Look at Lowering Premiums

As with just about any insurance program, options for lowering premiums are available. The trade-off is less indemnity. For example, there are plans that only cover facility-based care. Others are more comprehensive and, therefore, cost a bit more. It is important to step back and look at long-term care insurance globally and understand what types of coverage are available. Decide whether you want the more comprehensive plans or if you want to "hedge your bets," so to speak, and only cover facility-based care, such as nursing homes and assisted living. Essentially, all companies that offer LTC insurance define the types of coverage with the same language. When you are putting a plan together, you can decide whether to have all the benefits, the "bare-bones" coverage, or somewhere in between.

The Physician's Role

If you do have an insurance policy or a hybrid Life/LTC policy, who decides whether you qualify for benefits under your plan? Your doctor does. Who determines whether or not you go onto claim? Your doctor does. The insurance company will require that a physician certify that you are unable to perform the required number of ADLs as specified in your policy. Typically, to qualify for benefits, you must be unable to perform two of the six ADLs. The good news is that the insured's inability to, say, eat or dress does not have to be caused by a specific illness. It can be illness-related, accident-related, or just because of the normal aging process. Claims are paid according to the terms of your policy once your doctor makes his determination and certifies it in writing. This is true regardless of what type of insurance plan you select, whether it is the original long-term care insurance or the hybrid Life/LTC policies.

Taxation

The looming tidal wave of 70 million retiring baby boomers has prompted federal and state governments to sweeten the long-term care deal by offering tax incentives to those who purchase long-term care insurance, hoping to lessen the potential drain on Medicaid resources. But there are a few things that you need to know about LTC insurance as it relates to taxes. First, benefits received under a qualified long-term care policy are typically free of federal income tax free, and usually free of state income tax too. Why? Because they are regarded by the government as insurance reimbursements for medical expenses. The tax-free cap is adjusted annually for inflation. Even if you receive benefits above the cap, they are still free of federal income tax as long as they don't exceed your actual long-term care costs. If you collect LTC insurance benefits during the year, that amount should be reported to you on Form 1099-LTC, which you should receive early in the following year. You then calculate the taxable amount of benefits (hopefully zero) on Form 8853, which you should attach to your Form 1040.[19]

---

[19] American Association for Long-Term Care Insurance. "1099 LTC – IRS Form Reporting Long Term Care Insurance Benefit Payments Understanding

The tax advantages are significant if you are self-employed. Instead of listing your LTC premiums on Schedule A, they go directly on line 29 ("Self-employed health insurance deduction") on Form 1040. That way it comes right off the top of your income. (Laws may vary by region. Consult your tax professional for details.)

Qualified long-term care policies are eligible for federal income tax breaks. And, depending on where you live, they may be eligible for state income tax breaks as well. The key lies in understanding what the word "qualified" means in the eyes of the IRS. Qualified policies must be guaranteed renewable and they cannot have any cash value. "Guaranteed renewable" means that the insurer is required to give you the opportunity to renew your policy when it expires. Most policies sold these days are qualified policies. Consult your tax professional to make sure.

Underwritten Options:
Original Long-Term Care Insurance and the Hybrids

Let's first explore the LTC options that require you to pass an underwriting exam and have the taxation and claim processes as described above. To qualify for the underwritten options, your health needs to be average to above average. Remember, insurance companies that offer these types of coverage are in it for the long haul and are very particular about who they offer coverage to. If you are in good health, you can consider all the options. If you are not, do not fret. There are non-underwritten options that I will explain later in the book. But if you are in relatively good health, here are your alternatives:

IRS Form 1099 LTC." http://www.aaltci.org/long-term-care-insurance/learning-center/1099-LTC-tax-reporting-long-term-care.php

Traditional LTC insurance may be a good option for you if you are income-rich but cash-poor, or if your main asset is real estate. Some combine traditional LTC insurance with Medicaid planning. This is where you hold the policy for the "look-back" period. Once the assets transfer into an irrevocable trust, you can drop the LTC policy. If you use this strategy, it is advisable to seek the assistance of a retirement advisor who is also capable of helping you with your overall retirement planning. It can become a bit more complex than I can detail in this book. Just know that the option exists.

The hybrid life/LTC insurance is gaining ground as a solution to paying for long-term care. Not surprisingly, many folks just were not impressed with the "use it or lose it" approach of traditional LTC insurance. You can almost see people's eyes bug out at the thought of paying from $6,000 to $10,000 per year for insurance they may never need. Add 20 years' worth of those premiums together and you have a tidy sum.

It doesn't take the insurance industry very long to react to public opinion. When it discovered that LTC policies weren't selling, the actuaries and computer jockeys who design insurance products went to work. They looked at the old standby life insurance, LTC's older brother. Here, they observed, was a product that had been around for centuries, had a solid claims reputation, and enjoyed a good history of not raising premiums. So, as the story goes, two family members got together over a cup of coffee and decided to launch the hybrid life/long-term care insurance that their product engineers had designed.

Why? What could a combined plan do?

A combined plan could answer the biggest nagging question that the people had. The answer to "What if I never need the care?" was "death benefit." The new hybrid programs would have a death benefit value, which meant that if the insured never needed care, then a tax-free death benefit would go to the beneficiaries. Suddenly, a plan that had no tangible value if it was never used now had real value. It also had a large sum that would be delivered tax-free and probate-free to the insured's heirs.

How do these plans work?

These hybrid policies have two pools of benefits: one for long-term care and one for life insurance. Some programs still have the two pools of benefits but vary in terms of what they emphasize. Some plans are slanted more toward LTC and others are slanted more toward life insurance. Other plans balance the two benefit pools, giving each aspect equal emphasis.

The other large difference between the Life/LTC policies is how they are funded. Some policies are funded with one, single lump sum premium, which results in what is called a "paid up" policy, others are funded with a monthly premium, and yet others are a combination where they are paid up in 10 years. Let's explore the single-premium options first.

Single premium options offer two benefits that are striking and set this option apart from the monthly funded options: (1) it becomes fully paid and there is no need for additional funds; (2) the premium paid is fully liquid and can be called in if necessary. Sometimes, these will be marketed as a savings account with a long-term care and life benefit. This is because the only loss to a policyholder when he or she liquidates the account is the interest; you can structure certain plans to have the interest paid to you but this option does have an impact on benefits. For the purposes of this example, let's look at one where you would lose the interest if you surrendered the policy. If $100,000 goes in, and then five years later you need the money, you would receive $100,000. You would miss out on the interest that would have accrued during that time. If interest rates are low, as they are at the time this book is being written, there is not much of a downside. If you have the money to park in a Life/LTC policy, and then later withdrew it and forfeited the gains, you won't have that much to lose if interest rates are low.

Following is an example of how it would work.

For a male, nonsmoker, 59 years old, $250,000 deposit, there would be three buckets:

- $250,000 is fully available for emergency purposes
- $1.276 million would be available for long-term care purposes
- $425,000 would be paid tax free as a death benefit if long-term care is never needed

How about a female, 59 years old, nonsmoker, and a $250,000 deposit?

- $250,000 is fully liquid at any time
- $1.285 million is in the long-term care bucket
- $429,000 is in the life insurance bucket

Both polices would pay after you were deemed unable to perform two of the six ADLs. Both policies would pay for nursing home care, home health care, and assisted living facilities. Both policies' benefits would be reduced by what you used, if you used any of the benefits at all.

Let's say, for example, that you used only $60,000 of LTC benefits. The life insurance bucket would be reduced by that amount, and then the remaining amount would go to the spouse or beneficiaries upon your death.

But what if your family does not have the $500,000 to put toward a Life/LTC policy? Then we would use the monthly funding strategy. The monthly funding strategies do not have the full return of premium that the single-deposit plans have, but they do have some residual value, and the death benefit and the long-term care benefit are exactly the same.

Let's take that same couple who did not have $500,000 to put down, but still wanted the Life/LTC insurance plans.

Male and female, both 59 years old, nonsmokers: Their $6,000 per year would buy $353,000 of total benefits for long-term care and life insurance purposes. Should either one of them become unable to perform two out of the six ADLs, they would be able to start drawing down the benefit on a monthly basis. Should either one of them die, the remainder goes to beneficiaries.

The way these policies work, if you never need the long-term care, then the full amount of the death benefit is paid tax-free to your spouse when you pass. Sometimes clients will draw down their IRA money and use their distribution to fund these types of policies for both LTC purposes and for tax purposes.

Innumerable possibilities exist when you combine different types of strategies to provide the multifaceted answers to such gaps.

Non-Underwritten Policies: A Self-Insurance Foundation

Medical underwriting is a health insurance term referring to the use of medical or health information in the evaluation of an applicant for coverage. Insurance companies must evaluate their risk in order to provide coverage or they would go out of business. They are gauging your health to make two decisions: whether to offer or deny coverage, and what premium rate to set for the policy.

Now, the big questions: "What if I can't qualify because of my health?" or "I have so much saved why bother with insurance, I'll just use my assets?" Whether it is traditional LTC insurance or the hybrid Life/LTC insurance policies, both require underwriting because of the possible large payout by the insurance company if you should need the care. But what if you are in poor health and uninsurable? What if you have a history of heart disease, diabetes, or cancer? There's good news.

The insurance industry has come up with another way of planning for long-term care by designing another hybrid product that is known as the LTC/fixed annuity. Similar to single-premium plans, this product requires a significant upfront deposit to make it strong enough to cover health care costs. But there are other uses for this product.

Just like the underwritten combination policies have a life insurance component, the non-underwritten "combos," as they are called by those in the insurance industry, have a traditional fixed annuity component, which is all about income, income, income. In other words, anyone who is considering a traditional fixed annuity for part of the guaranteed income portion of his or her portfolio now has the appealing bonus of an LTC component. This is a very positive trend in the world of insurance that scratches just where a lot of people itch.

Income riders: You can now add what are called "income riders" to annuities, whether they are fixed or variable. These income riders guarantee a certain rate of return, regardless of the performance of equities (on which the return of variable annuities is based), the interest rate environment (upon which the return of traditional fixed annuities is based) or the capped index strategies (upon which fixed indexed annuities is based). While the account defers, or "cooks," you receive this guaranteed rate, which can range anywhere from 4 percent to 7 percent, depending on the contract chosen. The catch is that to capitalize on this guaranteed interest rate, you have to annuitize and take the value over a lifetime. The lifetime payout can be set up so that it pays on one life or on joint lives, with the remainder of the account passing on to a beneficiary. These income riders have been available for at least a decade at the time this book is being written and have been a very popular way of setting up a stable retirement income that is hedged for inflation and will supplement Social Security (more on this later). Remember too, that the guaranties provided are based on the financial strength of the issuing company, so make sure that you are comfortable with the insurance company behind it.

Assuming we are in comfortable with the company, what has been truly revolutionary is the fact that in the past few years the insurance companies have added an LTC benefit to those same payouts. Now, when a client who is receiving a lifetime income payment is unable to perform two out of the six ADLs, or is confined to a nursing home, the income amount doubles.

Here is how it works: John Doe is 55 and has $600,000 in a 401(k) from a job he recently left, and he elects to invest in a fixed indexed annuity with an income rider that includes an LTC component. He plans on working and does not need the income, so he elects to defer the income for 15 years until he turns 70. At age 70 ½, he will be forced to make withdrawals from the account anyway due to the required minimum distribution rules set up by the IRS for tax-deferred accounts.

Fixed Index Annuity Payout with LTC Doubler	
Original Value	$600,000
Income Account Value (After 15 Years)	$2,419,719
Option A Fixed Annual Payout	$130,665 (5.4% of Income Account)
Option B Increasing Annual Payout	$106,467 (4.4% of Income Account)
LTC Doubler (2x Annual Payout)	$261,330 (Opt A) or $212,935 (Opt B)

Not only does John have the $130,000 per year to live on and to supplement Social Security, he also has the peace of mind of knowing that his lifetime payment doubles if he is unable to perform two out of the six ADLs mentioned earlier in this chapter. So now he can use the $261,330 per year to cover the costs of long-term care, whether at a nursing home, assisted living facility, or potentially home health care.

As you can tell, there are certain factors that enhance this planning tool and make it even more effective, such as making a larger deposit or allowing additional time to defer. The features and benefits of the product also vary by state.

This option is relatively new on the retirement and long-term care planning scene. The best feature of it is that no medical underwriting is required. This should be of special interest for those who have been turned down for either traditional LTC insurance or Life/LTC insurance or have elected to self-insure. They now have a place to park money to use for LTC purposes, or for income purposes. Perhaps the best part of all is that if they never use it for income or for long-term care, the full amount goes to beneficiaries and avoids probate. In that respect, it performs just like any other annuity.

Conclusion

The gap in LTC costs is enormous and only growing, and the federal government is making it harder and harder to qualify for assistance. What was once a three-year look-back period is now five years. What was once a penalty that was time-stamped is now retroactive and pushed into the future.

Compounding the situation is the "good problem" of increased longevity through medical technology. The number of people lining up for long-term care is multiplying, and we have not yet even seen the baby boom wave crash onto the LTC scene. Discover magazine called it the "Gray Tsunami," stating that by 2050, the number of people in the world age 80 and older will quadruple.[20]

That will trigger a financial emergency of immense proportions, with an unprecedented number of people needing expensive long-

---

[20] Wheelwright, Jeff. Discover Magazine. September 18, 2012. "The Gray Tsunami." http://discovermagazine.com/2012/oct/20-the-gray-tsunami

term care that they, their children, their grandchildren, and the government will not be prepared to pay for. Thankfully, as is usually the case, the private sector has sprung into action and is delivering alternatives and strategies that are redefining how people plan for that care, regardless of their health status, financial status, or disposition toward paying premiums and getting nothing in return. Regardless of what strategy you choose, the bottom line is this: choose one. Or, as I mentioned before, do it and do it early. The clock is ticking, and no one I know of is getting any younger. There will never be a better time to break out some of the new tools that have expanded our options in addressing the LTC gap.

CHAPTER 7

Minding the Income Gap with Modern Planning

"If you don't know where you're going, be careful. You might not get there."
– Yogi Berra

You're nearing 60 years of age. You're considering retirement. You just got that statement in the mail from the government that tells you what your Social Security income is likely to be. You have your calculator out and you are calculating your income against your bills and expenses. As you crunch the numbers, you are forming a picture of your desired lifestyle and comparing it to reality.

As we analyzed in a previous chapter, you will make a decision as to when to take your Social Security income. That decision will be, as we have discussed, based on your health, the "break-even age," your inclination to continue working, taxation, and spousal benefits, if married. That gives you some idea of how much your lifetime income from Social Security will be. But we are left with a gap — the gap between Social Security income and your mortgage, your health insurance, your plans for travel, and your hobbies. So that is the question, then, isn't it? What should you do about that gap?

For the record, this is an extremely difficult question to answer in a sentence or two. It requires more than the broad brushstrokes I am using here. Unlike questions having to do with Medicare and long-term care and when to take our Social Security, options having to do with filling in retirement income gaps are infinite and unlimited. At times, there are so many options for investment and withdrawals that it can be overwhelming and discouraging. People don't want to make mistakes, especially with retirement. Usually, there is one retirement, one chance, and no one wants to screw it up. The idea of having to put the work boots or work shoes back on and having to go back to the boss, hat-in-hand, is a situation that clients want to avoid. Or the idea of still being in their mid-70s and out of money doesn't work either.

There are only so many Medicare plans, and there are only so many long-term care strategies. There are also only so many ages to begin taking Social Security income, although it is important to remember that the cap is age 70. You must start taking it by then. With those fundamental decisions, we can drill down to all of the answers that apply. Meanwhile, the gap between your Social Security income and your expenses and your lifestyle is a broader topic with varying options for both investments and spending. I will offer a few solutions here, but they will by no means tell the full story. The reason? Because every individual case is different and there is no one-size-fits-all solution. My advice is to be wary of anyone who indicates that there is a one-size-fits-all solution. He or she is usually trying to sell you something. A professional financial advisor will begin by listening, taking thorough notes, and asking questions until he or she fully understands where you are, what you have to work with, where you want to go, and how much risk you want to take to get there. Like I said, no one I know of has the same picture in that regards — no one. A trusted, competent financial advisor should be able, however, to help you find a solution that is right for you and your family.

Understand Your Starting Point

Most folks are going to have a significant gap between their Social Security income and their expenses. Some will have paid for their homes by retirement age. But, believe it or not, most retirees will still be paying off a mortgage and will be responsible for property tax as well. When it comes to health care coverage, Medicare will apply by age 65, but Medicare doesn't pay for everything, as we have already discussed in previous chapters. There are health insurance premiums for Medicare supplement policies, bills for medicines that aren't covered under Medicare, and other such "gap" expenses.

When it comes to planning for retirement, one of the first and most important steps is to develop a budget and decide on an annual income that you will be satisfied with. Many who would not hesitate to take a frank look at their health and take steps to ensure that they live as long as possible will not do the same with their money. I am suggesting that you do some straightforward calculations with your annual income and ask yourself the following questions:

a.) How much do I need?
b.) How much would I like to have?
c.) What will inflation do to my income?
d.) What will the impact of capital gains and income taxes have on my income both now and in the future?
e.) How will aging affect my income?
f.) Will I outlive my assets?

How Much Do I Need?

I've always loved the saying, "Understand the difference between needing something and wanting something." This most definitely holds true when it comes to planning for one's retirement.

Whenever I sit down with clients, I start with their needs. They need a place to live and all the necessary utilities to keep that home up and running. They need health insurance. They need food. They need gas money and car insurance. They need reserve money — a liquid cash account to have on hand in case a roof goes, a boiler blows, the car quits — that sort of thing. When you start to answer the "how much" question, you start by making a tally of your requirements.

In actuality, you only need four things to survive:

- A roof over your head
- Enough food and water to maintain your health
- Basic health care and hygiene products
- Clothing (just what you need to remain comfortable and appropriately dressed)

Everything that goes beyond this — a big house, leaving behind a legacy for the next generation, name-brand clothes, travel, fancy foods and drinks, a new car — is a want.

That sounds simple and academic, doesn't it? And it is until we begin justifying and rationalizing. Let's face it: We're human. The line between needs and wants begins to blur when we are tempted to cross it. For example, your old car runs fine and gets you from point A to point B, but you pass by that new car dealership every day. One day you pull in just to check out the new models. You're just going to look. The salesman knows just how to push your hot button.

"Just sit behind the wheel," he purrs. That new car smell hits you. It wafts up and strikes your olfactory senses like narcosis and goes straight to your brain — the center for logical thought — and scrambles all its circuitry. You are now thinking with your eyes, your nose and your fingers as you revel in the elaborate upholstery.

"Transportation is a need," you say to yourself.

Yes, but ... who's fooling who here? You can't afford the new car. Buy it and you will not fulfill your other obligations and goals.

This is the crossroads where you either pass or fail the wants/needs test. The difference between a need and a want is pretty clear until you set yourself loose in a megastore and wander over to the electronics section. It's like knowing that you need to watch your weight and stroll into a fudge factory.

My point is that it is easier said than done. The people who are most successful at this part of the process are the ones who identify needs in writing, budget for them, and give no ground to temptation.

How Much Would I Like to Have?

Wants are so much more fun to talk about than needs. Now we are not just talking about staying alive, we are talking about lifestyle. And that is OK to do, once we have assessed our needs and have them cared for.

Some people call it "play money." Some call it "mad money." The idea is to look at all of your hobbies, interests, passions, sports, plans for legacy, travel goals, whatever it is that you like to do – or would like to do if you had the money – and put that down, too. I recommend that you give this some careful thought and be reasonable. Categorize everything you write down and then sort them in ascending order, according to what is most realistic and doable. Sure, maybe you would like to cruise around the world on your own private yacht. For most of us that would fall into the category of dreams instead of wants.

Part of this exercise is to determine where you wish to spend your retirement. For some there is no place like home. That's where things are most comfortable for you, and it may be where the grandkids live. For others, home may be what they wish to escape from. Perhaps they would like to live at the beach, or in the mountains.

Do you see yourself living in Cape Cod? Florida? California? Do you want to spend your winters in the South and your summers in the North? Write it down if it is a realistic want. This plays an important role in the planning process. We are often more motivated to save toward our retirement goals by focusing on wants rather than needs.

It's important to come up with a budget number for your wants. When it comes to planning, you have to work with numbers; otherwise it's not planning, it's hoping. If you place a want on your list, and it is something that you could never achieve, do, enjoy, or accomplish unless you won the lottery, you are wasting valuable planning time. Cross it off. Don't worry; you can always put it back on the list if your circumstances change. But for planning purposes, let's be as realistic as possible when developing our budget and the ultimate income goal.

What Will Inflation Do to My Income?

A safe bet on inflation is 3 percent. In the past, it has been more than 3 percent, and at other times it has been a little less, but when considering your income needs and wants, add 3 percent to whatever number you come up with to accommodate inflation. That's the point.

What many have discovered over the span of their retirement years is that because of inflation, the gap between their Social Security income and their desired income gets wider and wider as the years go by. Inflation is a threat to our real net worth and we need to prepare for it in our planning. As this is written, we are experiencing a time of low inflation. That could change. Some have made dire predictions in that regard.

"After years of low inflation, some investors seem to think it won't return," said U.S. News and World Report in an article that appeared February 1, 2018. The article, written by financial observer Debbie Carlson, went on to offer the view that complacent investors who are not prepared for inflation could be caught unawares by what she calls its "inevitable return."[21]

Inflation is like a forest fire. One minute it is not there, but the conditions are right for it to erupt. Then the next minute it strikes. When it does strike, it roars, sometimes to double digits, and feeds on itself.

In the late 1970s, for example, inflation reared its ugly head and gave the U.S. economy a royal spanking. By 1979, inflation had reached a startling 11.3 percent, and in 1980 it had soared to 13.5 percent. Food prices, rent, fuel prices... everything went up. People virtually stopped buying big ticket items they would be required to finance. The economic landscape was like a tinderbox, just right for an inflation fire, thanks largely to the unfettered U.S. dollar, which was no longer tied to the gold standard.[22]

Other contributing factors to the inflation wildfire of the 1970s were the shock of an oil shortage (whether real, or imagined,

---

[21] Carlson, Debbie. US News & World Report. February 1, 2018. "Are Markets Too Complacent About Inflation?"
https://money.usnews.com/investing/investing-101/articles/2018-02-01/are-markets-too-complacent-about-inflation
[22] U.S. Inflation Calculator. "Historical Inflation Rates: 1914-2018."
http://www.usinflationcalculator.com/inflation/historical-inflation-rate

doesn't matter) and an earlier wage and price freeze, just to name two. But that's the way it usually happens with inflation.

If there is any silver lining in an inflation shock like the one experienced in the late 1970s, it is that it is usually followed by a brief and deep recession, which resets the machine until something else comes along and tears it up and we begin again. Additionally, it is one of the stated goals of the Federal Reserve to keep inflation as close to 2 percent as possible and will raise interest rates as needed to keep inflation in check.

The point is, don't be lulled into complacency, thinking that you won't be affected by inflation during your retirement or that inflation will stay as low as it has been over the recent history. What will inflation do to your income? No one really knows since inflation also affects different products in different ways. Think of your health insurance. That seems to increase quite a lot while your cell phone bill may have been flat for long periods of time. Conservatively figure on 3 percent just to be somewhat prepared. Logically, just because we can't predict, account for, and prepare ourselves completely for every possible contingency doesn't mean that we should not be as prepared for as many as we can foresee. Consider using 3 percent in your calculations and then plan accordingly.

How Will Taxes Affect My Income?

Back in the world of Greek mythology, there existed a three-headed dog named Cerberus who had a serpent for a tail and guarded the gates of Hell. Thankfully, the IRS is not as fearsome as this monster described in the history books, but it does bite in three ways: income taxes, capital gains taxes, and estate taxes. For the purposes of income, we'll briefly focus on income taxes and capital gains.

Most people are generally aware of these terms, but it is good to know that there are two different tax rates applied depending on the source of the money. For example, was it earned from a job or, more importantly in this case, withdrawn from an IRA or 401(k)? That money is subject to income taxes. Was the money earned from the sale of stocks or the sale of property? That is subject to capital gains.

When you begin to plan on the sources of income to bridge your income gap, you need to consider how much the IRS will take before you can spend the money freely. The good news about IRAs, 401(k)s and 403(b)s, and all of the other retirement savings programs, is that they allowed you to write off what you contributed into the plan during all of those working years. The bad news is that Uncle Sam eventually wants his pound of flesh. Since these retirement savings programs make up most Americans' plans for retirement, understanding how much goes to the government and how much goes into your pocket is critical.

The intricacies of tax planning are too broad a subject to include in a brief study of income planning but here are a couple items of note:

a.) Income taxes are progressive, which means the more you withdraw, the more taxes you pay.

b.) Capital gains taxes are a flat rate.[23]

What this means is that if we can get more money under the capital gain tax system as compared to the income tax system, there is potential tax savings. Think of it as that head of Cerberus doesn't bite as hard as the income tax head. There are many ways to accomplish this whether it is considering contributing to ROTH

---

[23] There can be additional surcharges for higher income earners of up to 3.8 percent.

IRAs or after-tax dollars while working, or ROTH conversions after retirement, but creating tax diversification is as important as investment diversification.

When planning for your retirement income, we need to estimate what our tax liability will be so that the net amount – the amount after taxes – will cover the needs, the wants, the inflation and the other considerations below. Remember, state taxes are all specific to your residency. Also, always consult with a tax professional to understand how your retirement income will be affected by Uncle Sam.

How Will Aging Affect My Income?

Without rehashing the long-term care discussion that appeared in earlier chapters of this book, gerontologists like to classify people into three categories: "young old," "old," and "old old." This is very helpful to know, because your income desires will naturally decline with age. Your inclination to travel, indulge your hobbies, and pursue your favorite pastimes, especially those requiring an output of energy, will lessen in your 80s compared to what it was in your 60s. While that is going on, however, your health care situation may change. As you age you will probably need more medicines to keep yourself going, and your need for medical services will probably increase. Hopefully, financial planning professionals will have made sure you are covered for health care contingencies to the fullest extent possible.

Will I Outlive My Assets?

What would you say older Americans fear most? Death, or outliving their assets? According to MarketWatch, an online personal finance magazine, the No. 1 thing that scares people about retirement is running out of money.

"Older Americans' No. 1 fear about their retirement is that they won't have enough money to afford retirement," said the article, entitled "Older People Fear This More than Death." It continued, "... Outliving their savings and investments, making that the top fear — over loneliness, boredom and even declining health, among other fears, according to a survey of more than 2,000 workers ages 50 and older released in December [2015] by the Transamerica Center for Retirement Studies."[24]

Older Americans are growing more and more nervous because many who were depending on their 401(k)s and other invested retirement savings to see them through their golden years experienced dramatic losses in the 2008 economic downturn. According to one AARP survey, 53 percent of those polled said they saw their net worth drop so significantly during the economic downturn that they decided to cut back on such things as dining out, traveling, and entertainment in an effort to recapture a portion of those losses.[25] In addition, as mentioned earlier, virtually no one wants to be forced out of retirement and try to re-enter the workforce in their later years.

So that is a legitimate question, isn't it? I've already addressed the biggest financial risk to savings, which is health care costs. Now that we have considered inflation, needs, wants, taxes and aging, it's time to move on to the income gap. We need to come up with a figure and then compare it with what Social Security is going to bring in.

---

[24] Hill, Catey. Marketwatch. July 21, 2016. "Older people fear this more than death." https://www.marketwatch.com/story/older-people-fear-this-more-than-death-2016-07-18

[25] Mackenzie, Sandy. AARP Public Policy Institute. December 19, 2008." The Impact of the Financial Crisis on Older Americans. https://assets.aarp.org/rgcenter/econ/i19_crisis.pdf

For example, Steve and Jane Smith, both 65, are on the verge of retirement. After using the income analysis above, they realize that they would like to have a combined annual income of $100,000 per year. Their combined Social Security income is going to bring in $48,000 per year. That means that the difference between their income goals and their two sources of income is $52,000 per year. We've identified Steve and Jane's income gap. Fortunately for them, they have about $1.5 million in IRAs and 401(k)s. However, that figure is a lump sum. How long it will last depends on two things: (a) what distribution strategy they put in place to stretch that number out over their lifetimes, and (b) how long they live. What should they do?

You would need a book the size of *War and Peace* to parse through all the strategies and philosophies out there that address this question. This is not that book. Frankly, it would be impossible to vet them all. But I will offer up two global suggestions here. The first will update you on a change in conventional wisdom, and the second is a brief introduction into three strategies that may or may not be ideal for you, but something that I believe is one of the most powerful planning tools around.

A Change in Conventional Wisdom

Have you ever heard of the 4 percent rule? For years, conventional wisdom held that if you withdrew 4 percent per year from your investment portfolio, you would not outlive your assets. What some folks would do is maintain a relatively well-diversified stocks and bonds portfolio, and then have their advisor send them 4 percent per year — the idea being that this would bridge the gap between their Social Security income and their desired income and would last them the rest of their lives. Sounds good, no? There's no way that your account wouldn't earn at least 4 percent, right? And even if it didn't, at that rate, taking out 4 percent per year, your account would at least last 25 years, right?[26]

Wrong.

Why not? Unfortunately, this conventional wisdom ran into the 2000s. The 4 percent strategy was one that had not been applied. It had been developed in the 1990s and had used projections that were based on recent experience in the stock market. Furthermore, it was a theory that was developed but was never applied, since it was research done on behalf of the baby boom generation, which had not begun to retire yet. When baby boomers began retiring and putting the 4 percent strategy to the test, it didn't work. Like so many ideas, it looked good on paper, but it just wouldn't fly. The 4 percent rule of retirement investing was created in 1994 by Bill Bengen, a financial advisor in California. The idea was for the portfolio to be invested in a typical stock/bond mix and be rebalanced as the years of 4 percent withdrawals went on. The problem was that the theory was based on projections and was not guaranteed.

It is my opinion that "ifs" and "maybes" are great for gambling, but not so good for retirement planning. You need guarantees. You don't want to rely on the stock market to finance that cruise you always wanted to take or to upgrade your car. Once the decade of the 2000s started, with its downturns and volatility, it became obvious that this vaunted 4 percent rule was obsolete. The problem, however, was that many stockbrokers and other non-fiduciary financial professionals still pushed the concept because it benefited them financially.

---

[26] Maranjian, Selena. The Motley Fool. November 12, 2017. "3 Serious Problems With the 4% Retirement Rule."
https://www.fool.com/retirement/2017/11/12/3-serious-problems-with-the-4-retirement-rule.aspx

Another of the theory's inherent flaws lay in the fact that downturns in the market are compounded losses. The 4 percent rule would have worked great if things were to have continued as they were in the 1990s, when the stock market was a constant onward and upward parade. But when the stock market is on a losing streak and you are withdrawing 4 percent from a losing account, your 4 percent withdrawal is going to be tacked on to the additional "withdrawal" forced upon you by those market losses.[27]

There is an old saying about how timing is everything. In retirement, it has a big impact and one that we need to do the best to control and plan for. Let's say a client retired in the early '90s, as Mr. Bengen was developing the 4 percent rule, and that client just enjoyed almost a full decade of a bull run and a stable retirement. Compare that to a client who retired in 2000 and faced 10 years in the 'lost decade,' which began with the Nasdaq bubble bursting and included the 2008 financial crisis to boot. We can't control when you want to leave your working career and the economic conditions at that time, but laying the groundwork one to five years before you put your notice in is a good start.

Reverse Dollar Cost Averaging

Going backward is huge when you are no longer contributing to an account but depleting it little by little for your paycheck. You run smack into something called "reverse dollar cost averaging." When you were younger and still in the accumulation stage of life, if you were making regular, systematic contributions into an investment

---

[27] Bernard, Tara Siegel. The New York Times. May 8, 2015. "New Math for Retirees and the 4% Withdrawal Rule."
https://www.nytimes.com/2015/05/09/your-money/some-new-math-for-the-4-percent-retirement-rule.html

portfolio, you actually benefitted from the ups and down of the market. It is a rule of investing known as "dollar cost averaging."[28]

Here's the way it worked: If the stock market was up, that was great. Your account balance was up, too. If the stock market was down, that was OK, too. Why? Because you were making regular contributions to an account that bought shares with each deposit you made. The shares were cheaper when the market was down. The key was to keep making those regular contributions to the account. With time on your side, you were able to smooth out the volatility no matter which way the market moved. But what helped you in the accumulation stage could now hurt you when you retired. Think about it. If you stop contributing to the account on a regular basis and now begin withdrawing on a regular basis, you are now selling shares out of your account, not buying them. If the market is down, and you take out 4 percent, and the market loses 4 percent, in essence you just withdrew 8 percent, didn't you? Now these may be offset by dividends but while the market falls, your bills don't stop coming in, and your expenses can't be put on hold. They continue apace. You must sell shares to keep the income coming in. What was that sound? It was you just getting run over by "reverse dollar cost averaging."

If you are consistently withdrawing 4 percent from an equity-based account, you must factor in market losses as being tacked onto your withdrawals. What was a normal 5 percent loss in a month became 9 percent once you factor in your 4 percent withdrawal. What was a 10 percent loss now becomes a 14 percent loss. While you have your slide rule out, calculate this: In a losing scenario, folks would have to earn 12 percent to overcome that loss of 9 percent and 18 percent to overcome that loss of 14 percent. And those days of double-digit returns seem to be long gone.

---

[28] Dollar cost averaging does not assure a profit or protect against a loss in declining markets.

Consider this statement from William Sharpe, a 1990 Nobel Prize winning economist: "Supporting a constant spending plan using a volatile investment policy is fundamentally flawed. A retiree using a 4 percent rule faces spending shortfall when risky investments underperform, may accumulate wasted surpluses when they outperform, and, in any case, could likely purchase exactly the same spending distributions more cheaply."[29]

In other words, if our "at-risk" funds underperform, we are in big trouble with the 4 percent rule.

---

[29] Sharpe, William. April 2008. "The 4 Percent Rule – At What Price?" https://web.stanford.edu/~wfsharpe/retecon/4percent.pdf

CHAPTER 8

Effective Income Solutions

"Never go to excess, but let moderation be your guide."
– Marcus Tullius Cicero

A Greek philosopher once said, "Everything in moderation." This ancient wisdom certainly holds true when it comes to ensuring that we don't run out of money in retirement. The three strategies that follow this wisdom are not new. Nor are they my invention. Nor are they mutually exclusive. I have many clients who blend the three concepts or borrow a little from each, but all can be very effective in filling the gap between Social Security income and the total income you need to support your needs and hopefully your wants as well.

Growth Vehicles, Income Vehicles

As you may have read in another book I co-authored entitled "SHP's Retirement Roadmap: Your Map to Financial Freedom," the first strategy that we'll explore is the breakdown of each asset into a pure and direct goal. We refer to this concept as the safety, income and growth model where every asset that you own should fall clearly into one of these three categories.

The concept is that when you boil down every investment, they normally have one primary goal. Once you have identified your goal or goals, you should use the most specialized asset within that category to meet that goal.

Let's take one asset class at a time.

Safety

The goal of this asset is to have liquid money ready for an emergency or travel or upcoming renovation. Think of your safety money as your 'rainy day' fund. Since everyone should have an emergency fund, what are the needs of this fund? Well, it needs to be liquid in the sense that we can access it quickly and it needs to be safe in the sense that we need to be sure the money is going to be there when the emergency strikes. What investments are fully liquid and are insured by the federal government? If you said checking or savings accounts, you're right!

Step one in this strategy is to identify exactly how much we would need in an emergency fund, which could be three to six months of expenses or more for comfort level and then shift that portion into the bank with FDIC protection.

Income

The goal of this asset is to bridge the gap in income that you will have upon retirement. For example, if you have an income goal of $8,000 per month and your Social Security is $3,000 per month, then your income gap is $5,000 per month. Which assets are designed for income? Unlike the safety funds, these answers begin to vary. Annuities, rental properties, bonds (corporate, government and high yield), dividend paying stocks, and REIT's (real estate investment trusts) are the first ones that come to mind, but you may have even come up with others.

Step two in this strategy is to decide how much risk you would like to take in meeting your income gap. In the example above, the income gap was $5,000 per month. If we wanted to build a conservative income plan we would consider a fixed annuity to meet this income gap. The good news is that a fixed annuity provides protection from market risk. However, since it is conservative, you would need to dedicate more of your total funds to meet the income gap. On the other hand, you may want to build a moderate income plan, which utilizes some corporate bonds and some REITs that have higher yields. However, there is more risk of loss associated with those investments. All in all, within the income category, you can move up and down the risk/reward scale to find your comfort level and then based on that comfort level, you would dedicate enough of your assets to produce the $5,000 per month.

Growth

The goal of these assets is long-term growth and is mainly invested in the stock market and growth stocks in particular. Because this is the asset class that takes on the most risk, you must be very comfortable with the volatility. However, if properly structured, the safety and income accounts would cover all of your needs and wants. Whatever goes into the growth category would truly be for the long term. Moreover, any major market loss in this group would not have an impact on your lifestyle because you have your income coming in.

Step 3 in this strategy looks like this: After you have established your safety account and income accounts, the remaining amount would go into the growth accounts which can be the most aggressive if it meets your long-term goals and risk tolerance.

That is the key principal of this strategy: By organizing your financial plan around these three categories, you buy yourself the time in the market for it to cycle through its highs and lows without overreacting at the wrong time.

Imagine a couple, Evan and Katie, both 64, recently retired from a local utility company. They have about $1.5 million combined in their 401(k)s and bank accounts. Their main goal was to live comfortably, rent an RV for cross-country trips, and not have to worry too much about the stock market. After we analyzed their expenses and compared them to their pension and Social Security amounts, there was a gap of $4,000 per month. Here's how their three accounts were structured through the 'safety, income and growth' model:

1. Safety - $100,000
    a. With the trip upcoming and for their own comfort level, they wanted to have a good chunk in cash for emergency purposes.
2. Income - $800,000
    a. They had a very low risk tolerance and elected to go with a fixed annuity instead of bonds or dividend paying stocks. Remember too, there are many types of fixed annuities, but modern annuities have a death benefit and protection against inflation.
3. Growth - $600,000
    a. Now that their income was guaranteed by the insurance company and they had their 'rainy day' fund established, the rest of the money was put into a moderately aggressive portfolio for long-term growth.

For some, it is the simplicity of this model that is most appealing. They may be leaving money on the table by taking less risk and there may be less flexibility, but it is easier to wrap your head around the concept.

Bucket Theory

Similar to the 'safety, income, growth' strategy, the bucket planning strategy begins by taking a hard look at your income gap and your personal budget. The difference is that rather than creating accounts that are based purely on their goals, the bucket theory separates them based purely on the time frame.

Much about financial planning, especially investment and income planning, is based on time horizons. Let's say you're 25 years old and you have a 50-year time horizon. You can be as aggressive as you want. If you're 75 and you have a two-year time horizon, the recommendation would be much different. The bucket theory follows that concept closely. Following is how it works.

Bucket One

After we have identified the income gap and set aside the emergency funds, we would plan out how much would be needed in five-year increments. Using the same example above, Evan and Katie would need $4,000 per month or $48,000 per year. Assuming two percent growth, they would need to set aside $226,000 from their retirement funds to meet the income gap for year one through year five. To achieve our two percent assumption, the $226,000 would be invested in conservative portfolios of short-term bonds and other conservative vehicles that would have low risk but some return in order to meet that particular goal.

Bucket Two

Once the first bucket is established and funded, we move on to bucket two. Here we must calculate the effect of inflation on the income gap, determine what a reasonable expected rate of return will be, and invest these funds in a blended stock and bond portfolio to reach that goal. In Evan and Katie's situation, we would need $53,000 per year to meet their income gap in years six through 10.

Assuming we earned 4 percent for five years, we would fund bucket two with $205,000. This would grow to $250,000 in five years, which would be enough to fund Evan and Katie's retirement for years six through 10.

Bucket Three

Same process, but now we're planning for years 10 through 15 and 15 through 20, etc. The longer we have before the money is needed, the more aggressive the portfolio becomes as it holds more stocks than bonds. Eventually, the $1.4 million which is not in the emergency fund would be assigned to a specific bucket with investments that match the time horizon and income needs.

Yr	Bucket 1	Income	Bucket 2	Income	Bucket 3	Income
1	$226,000	$48,000	$210,000	$ -	$964,000	$ -
2	$182,520	$48,000	$218,400	$ -	$1,012,200	$ -
3	$138,170	$48,000	$227,136	$ -	$1,062,810	$ -
4	$92,934	$48,000	$236,221	$ -	$1,115,951	$ -
5	$46,792	$48,000	$245,670	$ -	$1,171,748	$ -
6			$250,584	$53,000	$1,230,335	$ -
7			$202,595	$53,000	$1,291,852	$ -
8			$153,647	$53,000	$1,356,445	$ -
9			$103,720	$53,000	$1,424,267	$ -
10			$52,795	$53,000	$1,495,480	$ -
11					$1,525,390	$59,000
12					$1,496,898	$59,000
13					$1,467,836	$59,000
14					$1,438,192	$59,000
15					$1,407,956	$59,000
16					$1,377,115	$59,000

Moving forward, at each annual review, Evan and Katie would adjust the holdings in each bucket to reflect that a year has gone by and they need to make the later buckets more conservative as their time for distributions comes closer. This takes discipline but it can be done.

The bucket theory is similar to the 'safety, income, growth' theory which is to use time frame and the proper investment vehicles, but it differs in how it is organized. The bucket theory emphasizes flexibility but requires more risk tolerance and discipline.

Dividend Paying Stocks

For those of us who are lucky enough to have a smaller income gap or significant assets saved, there is the possibility to invest the retirement assets into blue chips, utilities and telecom stocks, or exchange-traded funds (ETFs), which would be enough to fill that gap.

In Evan and Katie's situation, they had $1.4 million that could be invested for their retirement income. With an income gap of $4,000 per month, they would need a portfolio of dividend paying stocks or funds which would need to clear 3.5 percent in dividends to meet their income gap.

Like most income planning, the first step is the same in identifying the income gap and then discussing the goals and risk tolerance of the client. The dividend paying stock plan is the most aggressive since we are relying on the companies to continue to pay the dividend through thick and thin. If there is a large market drop, it could cause great anxiety to watch the portfolio drop, even if the dividend income keeps flowing. On the other hand, if we have a strong risk tolerance and we are looking for that combination of steady income, and the most long-term growth, the dividend paying stock concept is a consideration.

Conclusion

So, Matt, Mr. CFP®, which one do you recommend? Which one do you like best? My answer: Whichever one the client likes best. As you can see, there are certain themes that do not change: understanding the goals of the client, identifying the income gap, reviewing a client's risk tolerance, confirming the client's time frame, and finally matching the correct investment to all of these variables.

Picking the correct income plan takes careful consideration and a thorough review with a financial professional. Hopefully by introducing some common strategies, you can enter those conversations with more confidence and find the right strategy for you.

CHAPTER 9

Wealth is in the Eye of the Beholder

"Wealth — any income that is at least one hundred dollars more a year than the income of one's wife."
— H.L. Mencken

Money is a very personal matter. As a kid growing up in Boston, I was taught that it wasn't good manners to ask someone how much money they made. According to my mother, it wasn't polite to put your elbows on the table, ask for anything without saying "please" and "thank you," and, for goodness' sake, you didn't come right out and ask someone how much money he or she made. It was too nosey and downright rude.

So here I am, 30 years later, being rude nearly every day. As a Certified Financial Planner™ and retirement advisor, I have to ask that question quite often, since income is one of the five key elements in financial planning. But people who come into my office expect that. It's like the doctor asking you how much you weigh. A question that may be considered rude and insensitive in polite conversation becomes quite acceptable in a doctor's office. After all, a doctor can't help or heal without first understanding the patient and finding out what the problem is. Similarly, a financial planner cannot help clients unless he understands them financially.

I often think of this medical metaphor when solving people's money problems. A competent and capable doctor will not prescribe any medication for a patient without first doing a thorough examination. It's the same, or at least it should be, with a financial advisor. I have had many come into my office for the first meeting with an armful of account statements.

"We will get to those in a few minutes," I usually tell them. "First let's get to know each other a little bit." This is a polite way of saying I want to know all I can about them — their hopes, their dreams, their goals, their hobbies and, most importantly, what money means to them. Believe me, it means something different to every individual who walks through my door.

I will never forget one man who came to my office. He had listened to our radio show and responded to a complimentary consultation. When he confirmed the appointment, I asked him to bring in all the pertinent information about his finances so that we could get an idea of where he was now and perhaps project where he wanted to go. He told me that he had put off coming to see me the way some people procrastinate on going to the doctor or dentist. No one wants to hear bad news.

"I'm terrible with money," he said as he sat down. He was tall and casually dressed and wore a Red Sox cap. I liked him instantly. He said he had just turned 55 and wondered how close he was to being able to retire. He had with him a battered briefcase, which contained several account statements and other financial documents. As it turns out, the man was quite wealthy and had very little debt. Considering his modest lifestyle, it was my conclusion that he could have retired twice over 10 years earlier. He really did not pay much attention to money. It meant little to him. It just wasn't how he kept score.

When he said that he wasn't a good manager of his money, he was telling the truth. He knew little about business, but he knew everything there was to know about his craft, which had to do with building and refurbishing boats. His work was of the highest quality, and he had a long list of satisfied customers. He had built his business over the years on word-of-mouth recommendations. With him, it wasn't about the money; he loved his work.

Some equate money with independence and security, especially when they approach retirement. One couple I spoke with shortly before the market crash of 2008 had $1 million combined in their 401(k) plans, and they were getting ready to retire. After we reviewed several of the income strategies, they decided to choose the 'safety, income, growth' program that would (a) keep their income sources safe from loss, (b) provide modest but steady growth, and (c) provide the confidence they needed when making the plunge into retirement. Their plan was on the conservative side of things, but they were passionate about safety and weren't interested in outperforming the stock market. They'd rather take less money over the long term because it came with less stress.

Who could have predicted that within months, the investments housed within their 401(k)s would fall so precipitously that, had they not repositioned their funds, they would have lost half their savings?

I am sure that when physicians help cure an illness with the knowledge, training and skills they possess, they feel rewarded merely by knowing they have fulfilled their Hippocratic Oath and succeeded in doing some good for their fellow man. When this couple called me after the stock market crash to say, "Thank you," it made me realize that helping someone protect his or her wealth is just as important as helping him or her acquire it. I credited the couple for their good sense and practical wisdom. When economic times are good and the stock market is pumping profits, some are blinded by the idea that it will never end. Another rule of thumb you may have heard of is the Rule of 100, which is to take your age and subtract it from 100. That is the amount you should have in stocks while the remaining amount should be fixed assets such as bonds, CDs or fixed annuities, which have a limited downside.

For example: Let's say you're 25, then 100-25=75. According to the Rule of 100, you should have 75 percent in stocks and 25 percent in fixed assets. If you're 75, then 100-75=25. You should only have 25 percent in stocks. Like the 4 percent rule, the Rule of 100 has its flaws and exceptions, but to say that you should manage your money more conservatively as you age is an understatement.

Wealth Means Different Things

Wealth means different things to different people. One thing I have learned not to do is judge. My job is just to help facilitate the goals of my client to the extent of my capabilities as long as they are within the bounds of what is ethical and legal. One couple with whom I met was dead serious when they told me that it was their desire to "spend every last cent" of their considerable wealth on themselves before they died. Have you seen the bumper stickers on the backs of travel trailers, campers, and motor homes that read, "We are spending our children's inheritance"? That was this couple. They were the quintessential early flower children who had done well in their family-owned real estate business. Their retirement picture was rock solid. They could meet their income gap with rental income, Social Security and dividend-paying stocks.

"Both our kids are professionals," explained the wife. "They are successful in their own right and they don't need our help." Leaving a legacy to heirs simply wasn't important to them. After setting up their retirement plan, which included income well beyond their expenses, anything left over was play money to them, and that's exactly what they were going to do with it. "We have worked hard and now we are going to play hard," said the man.

I have met others, however, who were almost self-punishing in the way they strove to leave as much behind for their children and grandchildren as possible. These individuals did without all their lives so they could pass on as much as possible to their families. People of that disposition are certainly to be commended for their selflessness, which I believe to be a virtue.

One couple with whom I met were both in good health and of average means. They were pleasantly surprised to see how they could use life insurance as a legacy tool, freeing up more for their own personal use in retirement. Sometimes, however, people who are inclined to be that selfless still find it difficult to enjoy their money without feeling an unwarranted pang of guilt. To them, thrift is like wearing an uncomfortable pair of shoes. They just can't get used to the idea that they somehow deserve some of the pleasures life can extend. In his book, "Stay Rich for Life," IRA expert and nationally-known television personality Ed Slott calls this the "martyr syndrome." He tells the story of a couple who had worked hard and saved more than $1 million, but wouldn't touch it because they wanted to leave it to their kids. He contends that there is really no need for that when life insurance companies would only charge between 4 percent and 10 percent of that amount to provide a life insurance policy with a face amount of $1 million![30]

"That way," he said, "you die, and your kids get more than you ever had, and it's all tax free!"

---

[30] Slott, Ed. February 24, 2009. "Stay Rich for Life! Growing & Protecting Your Money in Turbulent Times."

Found Money

If you have ever been rounding up clothes to take to the cleaners and found a $5 bill in a coat pocket, you know the feeling of coming across what I call "found money." As a Certified Financial Planner,™ one of my greatest pleasures is to find extra money for the folks I'm working with. No reward is greater than seeing their expressions change from a quizzical look to a look of surprise and then to a broad smile when they realize that they have more money than they thought they had. And now with a comprehensive financial plan, they also have the confidence to begin spending it. It usually happens after we have analyzed everything, accounted for lifetime income and all the contingencies, and cared for the family. Then, when there is money left over, it's like that $5 in the coat pocket, or, as I mentioned earlier, going to a doctor and being told that you have reversed the effects of aging.

The Things Money Can Do

During my years as a financial advisor I have observed that if you ask 10 different individuals what money means to them, you will get 10 different answers. Here is a list of some of them that have surfaced during interviews:

Freedom — Money spells freedom from many things, among them, poverty! Financial freedom also affords one the peace of mind that comes from knowing that we will not be a burden on others and that our basic needs will be attended to.

Respect — This one may not set well with you, but people tend to respect those who are well moneyed. The wealthy are at least shown respect by others; whether they always deserve it is another matter. Respect is one of the reasons why some people pursue wealth.

Power — You probably have someone in mind on this one. Money is one pathway to controlling others, or at least wielding an influence in their lives.

Possessions — Money can buy you things. Homes, cars, boats, clothes, jewelry, computers, high-tech toys — stuff in general.

Security — Which would make you feel safer: To be in a strange place with no friends, no credit cards, and $2 in your pocket? Or to be in a strange place with no friends, but with a wad of $100 bills and plenty of plastic?

Immortality — Nothing says "forever" like having a school or a bridge or a hospital wing named after you. If you aren't remembered, at least your name will be... for a time, anyway.

Education — Among the things that money can buy is information and knowledge. If you don't believe money can buy these things, just ask how much it costs to attend a four-year university.

Altruism — You know that good feeling you get when you do something for others to make the world a better place, even if just temporarily? Well, money can buy that feeling. Poverty does not engender philanthropy.

Understanding Wealth

"We are what we repeatedly do. Excellence, then, is not an act, but a habit."
– Aristotle

From where I observe the turning of the financial world, it appears that there are certain formulas for the acquisition of wealth that the rich have learned to employ that the rest do not. Is it true in all cases? Of course not! Some attain wealth by inheritance and others through blind luck. But for the most part, it can be said of wealth, whatever you perceive it to be, it can be achieved by following certain habits and rules of behavior.

Hard work — It is a fact of life that even someone who has a high income but poor wealth-building habits will never attain financial security. The world is full of examples of financial failures who made and consequently lost fortunes.

On the other side of the coin, the world is full of examples of individuals who plugged along in relatively low-paying jobs but, through their industry and thrift, eventually obtained wealth. They did this largely due to what "they repeatedly did," as Aristotle said in the quote above.

As a financial advisor, I have the pleasure of meeting people from all walks of life and with all sorts of financial situations. As a student at the University of Connecticut, I opted out of psychology courses, but I have always found human nature to be a fascinating thing to study. As a teenage student at Boston Latin School, I saw that there were plenty of students whose IQs were probably off the charts, but who earned average academic marks. There were also students whose IQs were probably average, but, through diligence and hard work, earned excellent grades. When it comes to building wealth, hard work often wins out over intelligence, luck and working some investment scheme.

You always hear about the $1 million lottery winners. You see them on the evening news, standing with reporters in front of their oversized check, vowing that their newfound riches will not change them one little bit. They will keep their job as a taxi driver because they love the smell of the cab and don't ever want to leave their friends down at the dispatch garage. But it seldom lasts, does it? Soon the money is burning a hole in their pockets. They are beset by friends they never knew they had, all of whom are looking for a handout. Before long, they are penniless. Not all of them end up that way, but, according to statistics, most of them do.

One survey was reported to have shown that out of 100 lottery winners whose cases were studied, more than 75 ended up either poor or back where they started within five years. I know what you're thinking. That wouldn't happen to me. Maybe not. You are reading this book. That shows some sensitivity to the issue at hand — understanding wealth and what it means to us individually.

As to how someone who receives the sudden gift of wealth can let it slip through his or her fingers, consider the case of Jack Whittaker. He was the West Virginia man who won one of the largest undivided lotteries in U.S. history — $315 million. His windfall was announced on Christmas Day 2002. He opted for the lump sum, and, after taxes, he pocketed $113 million. Today, he is broke. What happened?

Soon after he cashed the check, things started to go horribly wrong for Jack. His granddaughter died of a drug overdose. He hit the gambling halls in Atlantic City, New Jersey, and was soon sued for bouncing checks to cover his losses. He was arrested for drunken driving and ordered to check into a rehabilitation facility. His construction business was burglarized. His car was broken into while parked at a nightclub. Thieves made off with more than $500,000. He was sued by former friends for his alleged connection with the death of an 18-year-old boy who was a friend of his granddaughter. A gang of con artists used counterfeit checks to clean out what was left of Jack Whittaker's windfall.

Those things make the news. What doesn't create headlines is the story of the school teacher who worked hard for 40 years and managed to save $1 million on a salary of less than $50,000 per year. One of the reasons why you seldom hear of individuals who had to work hard for their fortunes squandering them is because they appreciate them. Hard work does that for you.

Living Within Your Means — That modesty is a virtue cannot be questioned. But the power of this quality of human behavior to produce great wealth on even a below-average income is unheralded. And it should be heralded! From where I watch the world, immodesty when it comes to spending is gaining ground on its antithetical counterpart. Even the government — scratch that —

particularly the government, seems to have been infected with a loss of appreciation for this virtue. I'm not sure, but I believe that if our founding fathers could see the national debt clock rolling up such unfathomable numbers, they would be up on one elbow, ready to turn over in their graves.

The trend toward "buy now and pay later" started after World War II. Until then, only houses were mortgaged. Everything else was paid for with cash. At first, charge cards, as they were known, were issued to loyal customers of large department stores to save paperwork when they charged purchases to their revolving charge accounts. Each store had its own card. The idea of a single card that could be used at multiple stores wouldn't come along until 1949.

As the story goes, Frank X. McNamara, head of Hamilton Credit Corporation, was having dinner with his attorney, Ralph Sneider, and Alfred Bloomingdale, of the family that started the famous store by the same name. They were dining at Major's Cabin Grill, located next to the Empire State Building in New York City. McNamara was complaining that one of his customers had borrowed some money but was unable to pay it back and the unusual circumstances surrounding it. It seems McNamara's customer had lent a number of his department store credit cards to his neighbors for an emergency. The arrangement was for them to pick up what they needed and pay him back, plus a little extra. As it turns out, however, the neighbors ran up bills on the charge cards and didn't pay the man back. That's what forced him to borrow money from Hamilton Credit Corporation.

That discussion set the tone for what happened next. When the check came, McNamara fished in his pockets for his wallet to pay the bill. He discovered to his embarrassment that he had left his wallet at home. Red-faced, he called his wife to have her bring him some money. But the kernel of an idea was born in McNamara's mind of having a single card that could be used at multiple locations.

All it required was for a company to be the middleman between the merchants and the consumer.

McNamara ran the idea past Sneider and Bloomingdale, and the three of them used their resources to start a new company in 1950 they called the Diners Club. Now, instead of having to carry several cards to buy merchandise and gasoline, they could carry one card, the Diners Club card. The Club would bill the customers and pay the merchants. No interest was charged. Interest-charging credit cards would come much later. Instead, the merchants who accepted the Diners Club card paid 7 percent for each transaction, and customers who qualified to own the card paid $3 per year for the privilege.

At first, it really was a club for diners. The first Diners Club credit card holders were friends and acquaintances of McNamara's. This elite group numbered fewer than 200 in 1950, and 14 restaurants accepted the card. To begin with, Diners Club cards weren't plastic. They were made of paper; the merchant wrote the card number down and submitted the slip to the club for payment. By the end of 1950, there were 20,000 card holders, and by the following year, the club was turning an annual profit of $60,000.

By 1958, competition came along in the form of the American Express credit card and Bank Americard (later renamed Visa). And now, as Paul Harvey used to say, you know the rest of the story.

Has the plastic revolution been a blessing or a curse? Properly used, consumer credit has proven to be a great convenience and a significant boon to commerce in general. The economy thrives when money is exchanged, and the use of credit cards by prospering Americans soon made this exchange a free-flowing river. Improperly used, however, the buy-now pay-later movement has fomented crippling debt and left in bankruptcy many who found it difficult to live within their means with easy credit so readily available. Consumer debt seems to be out of control and according to the Federal Reserve Bank of NY, Americans are carrying $830 billion in credit card debt. Many are paying the "minimum payment due," digging the debt hole deeper each month. What's worse is that this is coupled by the student loan debt of $1.38 trillion![31]

If an individual wants to live within his or her means, it is essential for him or her to learn to identify the difference between wants and needs (see chapters seven and eight). It is apparently more easily said than done.

Patience — Ah! Another virtue that many seekers of wealth don't seem to possess much of these days. Warren Buffet talks often of investor patience. His success is often the result of waiting patiently for the right time to buy a stock, or even a whole company. Mary Buffet, who was married to the famous investor's son, Peter, for 12 years, said about her father-in-law's purchase of Dairy Queen at age 58, "He probably wanted to buy it when he was eight years old, but it wasn't the right price." Patience dictates that slow and steady wins the race, not impatience and impulsiveness. Saving steadily and investing carefully trumps chasing the next Google, Microsoft or Apple dream with leveraged dollars.

Alfred Einstein is credited with saying that compound interest is the eighth wonder of the world. It's not that I disagree with the statement; I am just not so sure he actually said it. I have always wondered what the setting was that prompted the famous physicist to utter such profound financial wisdom. Nonetheless, if I had understood the power of compound interest when I was a kid growing up in Boston, I would have saved every nickel I ever wasted, and that amounts to a considerable number of nickels.

One of my favorite examples of the power of compound interest is the story involving New World founder and famous voyager Christopher Columbus and the penny. If Columbus had placed a single penny in a 6 percent interest-bearing account and had told

---

[31] Mayer, Brittney. CardRates.com. May 24, 2018. "2018 Credit Card Debt Statistics: Average US Debt." https://www.cardrates.com/advice/credit-card-debt-statistics/

someone to take the interest out every year, the value of the interest earned by 2005 would be almost 31 cents. But if he had placed the same penny into the same interest-bearing account and allowed the earned interest to remain in the account and compound — earning interest upon the interest — the resulting balance for 513 years would be $95,919,936,112. That's $95 billion!

Education — The worst kind of fool, it is said, is the one who doesn't know, and doesn't know that he doesn't know. Knowing we don't know everything about wealth, the acquisition of it, and the preservation of it is the first step to obtaining it.

In my tour of duty so far as a financial advisor, there have been a few occasions when I have had to fire myself. This occurs when I am dealing with a client who simply insists on taking a course of action that I know beyond a shadow of a doubt will result in a complete disaster for him or her financially. It doesn't mean that I no longer wish to advise him or her; it's just that I don't want to accept responsibility for an action that will have such irreversible negative consequences. It doesn't happen often. But when it does, it is usually because someone is influenced by the opinion of a close friend who is passing on some hot stock tip, or some get-in-on-the-ground-floor-before-it's-too-late, get-rich-quick advice that "just can't miss." I am no soothsayer, and I have no crystal ball, but I do know this: If it sounds too good to be true, it usually is. And while we are knee-deep in clichés, if it walks like a duck and quacks like a duck — it's a duck.

Financial education begins with learning lessons from the past. If you are nearing retirement age, for example, should you risk your life savings on the expected success of a volatile stock market? Lessons learned from those who did so, and in the process lost years of retirement security, would dictate "no."

One of the most profound statements ever to come from the Cold War was uttered by Ronald Reagan, when he made famous the three-word policy declaration, "Trust but verify." Reagan is credited with coining the phrase, but he actually learned it from Suzanne Massie, an expert on Russian culture who was part of Reagan's advisory circle in dealing with the now defunct Soviet Union.

"The Russians like to talk in proverbs," she told the president. "It would be nice for you to know some of them," and then she informed him that "trust but verify" was a favorite of the Russians. She even taught him how to say it in Russian. Reagan used the phrase frequently in 1987 during negotiations with the Soviet Union on the INF (Intermediate-Range Nuclear Forces) Treaty. When his counterpart, Soviet General Secretary Mikhail Gorbachev, responded, "You repeat that at every meeting," Reagan reportedly answered, "I like it."

While it loses a little in the translation, the phrase means, in essence, that while a source of information might be considered reliable, one should perform additional research to verify that such information is indeed accurate or trustworthy.

Does that ever hold true in the world of financial planning! Opinions regarding what we should do with our money are flying in the print and electronic media like feathers in a pillow fight these days. It may be tempting for us to just throw up our hands and conclude that no one knows anything, and that since that is the case we might as well wrap up our money, put it in plastic bags, and bury it in the back yard. But, as we have discussed earlier, just because there are so many opinions, it does not mean that some of them don't have merit. No, you should not trust everyone. That doesn't mean that you shouldn't trust anyone. That's where the education comes in.

Examine the relationship you have with a financial advisor before acting on his or her advice. Is he or she a fiduciary?

That's a fancy word we won't hear much during a dinner conversation. It means that the advisor's advice is given solely and completely with your interests in mind, and not those of him or herself. That doesn't mean that the financial advisor isn't compensated for giving advice to clients about their finances. It does mean, however, that he or she is registered and certified, and required by both ethical standards and federal law to represent you - not some brokerage house or insurance company - with the advice or recommendations given.

The word "fiduciary" comes from the Latin word fiduciarius, meaning "(holding) in trust"; and from fides, meaning "faith." A professional who serves in a fiduciary capacity for you will never pressure you into buying a product. A professional advisor will propose solutions irrespective of commission, profit or personal gain. He will always encourage you to do your homework before making any decision and verify through independent research any course of action involving money.

Those who have accumulated great wealth are usually those who have taken the time to educate themselves first.

Most of us in the professional financial services industry keep our ear to the ground for any new developments, products or strategies that we feel may benefit our clients. We take continuing education classes, review trade journals, and keep up-to-date on government regulations that affect our clients' portfolios. A lot can be learned that way. But attitude is what makes the big difference in effectiveness.

If you are looking for competent, professional help, avoid anyone with the "know-it-all" attitude. You know that syndrome when you see it, and it should be a red flag to you. There is always something new on the horizon to learn. The landscape of the financial services world is constantly changing and adapting to the needs of the people. It's when we stop knowing what we need to know that we stop learning and cease being effective stewards of our craft.

The habit of lifelong learning enables us to improve our investments as well as our lives. Many of the approaches you have read about in this book may be unfamiliar to you. That is because they are relatively new. Some of them are viable solutions to the gaps that we must mind if we are to be successful wealth builders. Learning about them is part of our financial education.

The older I get, the more I realize that learning is a process, not an event. As soon as we think we've got it all figured out, something comes along to dislodge us from such hubris and remind us of just how much there is yet to learn. Make learning a daily goal, and your finances will thank you for it.

Conclusion

Aristotle was not just a philosopher. He was a mathematician, botanist, biologist, astronomer, and a part-time military strategist for Alexander the Great. When he said that we are who we are because of what we repeatedly do, he probably put the emphasis on the word "repeatedly."

Wealth requires all the habits listed earlier in this chapter, such as hard work, patience, etc., to be working in concert, day after day. Unless we happen to wake one morning to learn that we have won the lottery, wealth is not the result of a single act, but the constant accumulation of wealth-building acts and educated decisions.

As the example of the lottery winners who end up broke proves, it is also important to determine what our values are when it comes to money. Otherwise we may end up accumulating money just for the sake of collecting it, the way some people are known to collect old string and other useless articles for no reason. Is it possible for someone to become so obsessed with the accumulation of wealth that they put it ahead of everything else — friends, family, even their own personal integrity? Of course, it is.

How sad that would be. Money has no value other than as a means to an end. Without that factor, cash is merely high-quality paper with distinctive markings, and account statements merely so many numbers on a page. Those truly successful at accumulating wealth will take the time to integrate their financial goals with their personal goals.

CHAPTER 10

Setting and Striving for Clearly Defined Financial Goals

"People with clear, written goals, accomplish far more in a shorter period of time than people without them could ever imagine.
– Brian Tracy, Motivational Speaker and Best-selling Author

While some individuals are natural goal setters who enjoy setting a time line and a horizon for which to strive, others may have difficulty thinking that way. One of my favorite quotes is the one by Zig Ziglar in his book, "See You at the Top," where his wit and insight lead him to say: "Don't be a wandering generality; be a meaningful specific." Zig's philosophy is that accomplishing anything in life is made better by setting goals and achieving them. In the book, he tells his own story of starting an exercise program to improve his health and lose weight. He began jogging. He said that his first "run" was exactly one block. He came across the "finish line" huffing and puffing. The next day he was determined to increase his distance, and he did. He ran exactly one block and one mailbox. By adding a predetermined number of mailboxes to his run each day, he was eventually up to his goal of three miles. These daily three-mile runs eventually caused him to reach his goal weight.

It's like that with our financial goals. To quote Ziglar once again, "By the inch, it's a cinch; by the mile, it's a trial." When young people look at what appears to them to be the monumental task of saving hundreds of thousands of dollars for their retirement, they may tend to postpone saving. The mountain looks just too difficult to climb. But if they could only walk a mile in the shoes of a financial advisor, they would come to understand the powerful impact compound interest can have on even a small amount of money regularly saved — just like Christopher Columbus's penny mentioned in the previous chapter.

Whether you are young or old, setting financial goals may involve tradeoffs. If you are young, you may have to pass up that expensive weekend ski trip with your friends so you can apply those dollars to the down payment on your first car. That's called a tradeoff. That's called sacrifice. If you want the wheels, you have to forfeit the trip with friends. When you approach retirement, you may have to forfeit an expensive vacation to keep on track with your retirement savings program.

It helps to make the money-saving goals non-negotiable. Make a contract with yourself not to dip into your retirement fund, regardless of the temptation. (Emergencies may arise. It is always advisable to have a separate emergency fund for these unexpected events.)

Developing a mental picture of the goal already attained is a great way to find motivation. If your mental picture of retirement involves travel, imagine yourself on those journeys. Visualize the white sand of the beaches. Try to see yourself in a hammock between two palm trees. If you are a golfer, what courses do you want to play? See yourself there. Whatever your goal is, build a mental picture of it and use that picture to help you either work for or sacrifice for that goal.

Cutting back on expenses may be a tradeoff. Working harder, or longer, may be a tradeoff.

Life in America is Like a Cafeteria

The story is told of an elderly grandfather who came to America from Eastern Europe sometime around the turn of the century. He was coming to join his family, who had made the same voyage years earlier and were now fully Americanized. After being processed at Ellis Island, the old man went to a cafeteria in New York City to get something to eat. He sat down at an empty table, as he would have done in the cafés back in the old country, and waited for someone to take his order. Of course, nobody did. Finally, a woman with a tray full of food sat down opposite him and told him how a cafeteria worked.

"You start at that end," she said. "Just go along the line and pick out what you want. At the other end they'll tell you how much you have to pay."

Later the grandfather would tell a friend: "I soon learned that's how everything works in America. Life's a cafeteria here. You can get anything you want as long as you are willing to pay the price. You'll never get it if you wait for someone to bring it to you. You have to get up and get it yourself."

Conclusion

In this book we have reviewed in much detail the Social Security program, Medicare, Medicaid, long-term care planning, and strategies for sound income planning. We have also touched on the questions you need to ask yourself when you are approaching your retirement age, or already retired, for that matter. We even took it a step further to discuss a possible solution as to how to manage the gap between your desired income (wants) and your required income (needs).

We considered how the evidence points to the fact that there are no silver bullets when it comes to financial planning and retirement, and there certainly aren't any crystal balls. When you are considering your options on the right time to begin taking your Social Security income or how to manage health care costs, the decision is a personal one based on your health, your anticipated lifespan, your finances, and those of your spouse and family. Consequently, the decision you make in nearly all areas of financial planning will, out of necessity, be unique to you. There is no cookie cutter program or one-size-fits-all.

The same holds true for income planning. How you bridge those gaps will be an individual choice. Everything is personal. Some will choose to use stocks. Some will choose to use municipal bonds. Some will choose to use annuities. Whatever decision you make, it should be made based on your own values and concepts about wealth, and it should be one with which you can feel content, comfortable and confident. You should be able to sleep through the night, not pace the floor with worry. I often talk about personality — do what matches yours. Once you have done your research and due diligence, make the financial decisions that feel right to you — because in the big scheme of things, that's all you really have.

Made in the USA
Columbia, SC
11 April 2019